S0-BOI-460

HOCKEY CARD STORIES

KEN REID

ecw press

Published by ECW Press
2120 Queen Street East, Suite 200
Toronto Ontario, Canada M4E 1E2
416-694-3348 / info@ecwpress.com

LIBRARY AND ARCHIVES CANADA
CATALOGUING IN PUBLICATION

Reid, Ken, 1974–, author
Hockey card stories : true tales from
your favourite players / Ken Reid.

Issued in print and electronic formats.
ISBN 978-1-77041-197-5 (pbk.)
978-1-77090-609-9 (PDF)
978-1-77090-608-2 (ePUB)

1. Hockey cards. 2. Hockey players
—Anecdotes. I. Title.

GV847.6.R45 2014   796.962075
C2014-902562-9   C2014-902563-7

Editor for the press: Michael Holmes
Cover design: Michel Vrana
Cover images: CSA-Archive/iStock Photo
Interior image: Gum © Georgios Kollidas/
Shutterstock

The publication of *Hockey Card Stories* has been generously supported by the Canada Council for the Arts which last year invested $157 million to bring the arts to Canadians throughout the country, and by the Ontario Arts Council (OAC), an agency of the Government of Ontario, which last year funded 1,793 individual artists and 1,076 organizations in 232 communities across Ontario, for a total of $52.1 million. We also acknowledge the financial support of the Government of Canada through the Canada Book Fund for our publishing activities, and the contribution of the Government of Ontario through the Ontario Book Publishing Tax Credit and the Ontario Media Development Corporation.

PRINTED AND BOUND IN CANADA

Printing: Marquis 5 4 3 2 1

To Ash and Jacoby

For as long as I can remember, I've been obsessed with hockey. For just about as long, I've been obsessed with hockey cards. Baseball cards too, but let's stay on the ice.

I remember getting a quarter from my grandfather and walking down Union Street in my hometown of Pictou to Mr. Fraser's store. For most six year olds, the debate

INTRODUCTION

between a 25 cent pack of hockey cards or 25 cents worth of candy was a tough one. For me, it was a no-brainer. I took the hockey cards, and not because they came with gum.

Fast-forward a few years and I'd load up on cards on a Saturday night at the Hector Arena canteen during a Pictou Mariners Junior C game. For 25 cents, or maybe it was 35 cents by that time, you could get 12 cards of your NHL heroes. Back in those days, you could only watch an NHL game on the tube on a Saturday night, but thanks to a pack of cards, you could hold pictures of your favourite players right in the palm of your hands anytime you wanted.

I kept all my cards in an old box that my Daoust 301 skates came in. I remember one day I was showing my mom my collection of Wayne Gretzky cards, she made a great point.

"Honey, you should protect those. They could be worth something one day," said Ma. I'm not sure how she knew this, but Mom was on to something.

I took all my Gretzkys and put them in Ziploc bags.

I guess that was the forerunner to all the protective plastic cases you see nowadays.

A few years later, my mom came back from spring training in Florida with a few baseball cards and a baseball card price guide. A price guide, for cards?! These things *were* worth something. I was 12 years old. I riffled through my box of baseball cards. I soon discovered my Roger Clemens rookie was worth $15.

What?

That's when it really began. I started scooping up cards at an epic rate. If baseball cards were worth something, hockey cards must be worth something too. Eventually I stumbled across a hockey card price guide. It turned out that my Steve Yzerman 1984–85 O-Pee-Chee rookie was worth two bucks.

So the hoarding took over. By the time the hockey and baseball card boom came around, we're talking 1990–92, when most other kids started collecting, I was already dealing. My brother and I would set up at shows, mostly in Halifax. Our mom even made us business cards. Because we were still collectors at heart, we'd mostly sell doubles, although I do remember unloading a Yzerman rookie at a flea market for two bucks. I'd like to have that one back.

By my senior year in high school, I was working in a card store, owned by my buddy Sandy MacKay. We also sold Heaton goalie equipment; it was solid stuff.

Like most guys, after high school it was time to move on from my card obsession. Though I still dabbled in it, the cards stayed back home as I moved on, first to college then around the country as my broadcasting career began.

As I climbed up the broadcast ladder, I always found it amusing when I would march into a practice and interview the guys who were pictured on the cards I used to collect.

Whenever I'd go home, I'd rifle through an old box of cards. I couldn't help but smile at all the memories. And as I got older and the cards got older, the players on those cards got older too.

I began to notice a few things that escaped the eye of a 10 year old. How come the uniform Mike Eaves is wearing looks like it's drawn in crayon? Why does Kevin Morrison have such a huge head of curly hair for a man with no natural curls?

It turns out I was not alone. Blogs about old cards started to pop up on the internet. Lots of people, it seemed, really liked their vintage cards, whether it was because of a sweet set of sideburns or a throwback jersey.

But what did the players think of their old pieces of cardboard? That is what I wanted to know. And one day I decided to find out for myself. I called up former Winnipeg Jet Joe Daley. I knew he would have some insight on his old cards since he now runs a card shop in Winnipeg. He had a lot to offer. He was very insightful and forthcoming, and he approached the whole thing with a great sense of humour.

Maybe I was on to something here. I figured if all went well I could keep calling up players, ask them about an old card of theirs, and one day collect my columns and maybe release a book. We can all dream, right?

Then I ran into my colleague Ian Mendes, who put me on to a literary agent. Much like the price guide had stumped me back in the day, this whole literary agent thing stumped me as well. "You tell a guy your idea and if he likes it he tries to sell it? Is that how it works?" I asked Ian. He confirmed that was pretty much the process.

That's how I came across Brian Wood, my literary agent. He liked the idea and I got to work, digging through some of my favourite cards and calling up dozens of former players. And here we are. I hope this book brings a smile to your face; just looking at the cards brought back a lot of great memories for me. And when you hear from the guys on the cardboard, it really puts things over the top.

What did Mike Krushelnyski think of the airbrush job O-Pee-Chee gave him after the Gretzky trade? You'll get the answer. If you think a mid-'70s perm on a man is awesome, wait until you find out what *wasn't* on the card. Surely the guys who look so mean on their hockey cards must be nice and mellow by now. Right? What about when you get your card and you're not even on it?

These are the stories of the players on your old hockey cards, from the players on your old hockey cards. These are *Hockey Card Stories*.

I hope you enjoy.

TERRY RUSKOWSKI 1976–77 OPC #38 (WHA)

1979–80 OPC #141

Eternal youth. For what seems like forever, man has sear-
ched for the fountain of youth. Epic tales, books and movies
have been written about it. As we all know, the beauty
industry practically lives off the promised miracle of anti-
aging. And then there's that whole plastic surgery thing. So
what does that have to do with a couple of Terry Ruskowski

Chapter One — STRIKE A POSE

cards from the 1970s? Back in the day, Terry Ruskowski discovered an anti-aging method of his own.

Two hockey cards three years apart, and Terry
Ruskowski didn't age a day. How did he do it, or rather
how did the card makers do it? It's simple really: two
cards, one photo.

Apparently for the '79–80 set, the card makers couldn't
get a picture of Ruskowski in his new Blackhawks digs, so
they did the next best thing and went with a nice tight shot
of him from his days as a rookie with Houston in the WHA.

"I didn't realize that," Ruskowski says, 35-plus years
later. "That is hilarious."

It is kind of fitting that this picture got used a couple
of times during Ruskowski's career. For a lot of players,
the simple task of posing for a card isn't something that
can be found in their memory bank. For Ruskowski, who
according to the back of his '79–80 O-Pee-Chee, stood
5-foot-10 and weighed 178 pounds, posing was a moment
he will never forget.

"I remember that so very, very well because I remember

we were going in for practice and a guy came and said, 'We're going to take pictures for hockey cards' and I'm going, 'You got to be kidding? I'm going to be on a hockey card? I can't believe this.' I was just flabbergasted. 'Wow! I'm going to be on a card.' I was pretty pumped."

For Ruskowski, who went on to rack up 1,356 PIMS in his NHL career, his first card was an "I made it" moment. "I'm going, 'Geez, I mean you're asking me? I'm here, you know I made it.' All the years of people telling me I couldn't do it because I was too small, and now they're asking me for a picture on a hockey card? That's exactly how I felt. I'm going, 'Wow, I think I made it.'"

That pose got double the exposure in '76–77 and '79–80. The only thing that changed was the spelling of Ruskowski's last name. The card makers traded a "w" for a "u" in his last name in the later card, but we'll let the error slide for now. Instead let's solve a real hockey card mystery.

These cards have the perfect '70s feel, made possible by what I call the "disco curtain." You can see it, in all its glittery goodness, right behind Ruskowski. What is that blue and glittering piece of awesomeness? It shows up on a ton of cards from the '70s. It has to be some kind of futuristic, disco background, right? It is time for Terry Ruskowski to solve a hockey card mystery, one that has been bugging me and, I am sure, countless others for years.

"Actually, it was a wall. That was our practice rink" is the simple answer. Wow, that was underwhelming—mystery solved! That blue glob is not a curtain; the photographers didn't haul an awesome disco-era background around with them. It is simply a wall at the Houston Aeros' old practice facility. But what about the glitter? "Got to be the light because it wasn't glitter, I guarantee ya." Turns out there were no special effects used to make this card.

Whatever, the results are perfect. So why not use the picture twice? It's pretty cool for a guy like Ruskowski who grew up ripping into packs of sports cards and who, like a lot of us, fell victim to the person most largely responsible for card disasters everywhere: Mom.

"I used to keep my baseball cards and hockey cards. And I had a whole pile of them downstairs in my house and when I left my mother threw them all away. I had some beauties, I had some great cards, I kept them in good shape. I could have been a very rich man by now."

Among the men in Ruskowski's old card collection was Gordie Howe. Fast-forward to Ruskowski's first year as a pro in Houston, and he found himself on the same team as Mr. Hockey. Their first meeting came in a hotel elevator.

"My roommate and I were going to the elevator and we're going up; we were having a pre-game meal. And all of a sudden, the door flew open to the elevator and in walks Gordie Howe and I didn't know what to say. I really didn't know what to say. I looked at my roommate and he looked at me, and we just had this stupid stunned look on our faces. And [Gordie] came in and instead of pressing the button, he said, 'Oh, you're going to go up to the top for the pre-game meal; you must be with the Aeros.' 'Yes, sir.' He says, 'Well, I'm Gordie Howe,' and I said, 'I know.'

"It was just incredible and I have so much respect, so much respect, for that man. You know, growing up and watching him play you have a lot of admiration, but when you actually play with him—oh my gosh! He's just an incredible, incredible human being."

During the twilight of his career, Ruskowski got to play with another of the game's greats, Mario Lemieux. How many players got to play with both Mr. Hockey and Mario the Magnificent?

"I think I'm the only guy that ever did that," recounts Ruskowski, also the only NHLer to ever be captain of four different NHL teams.

"How do you explain Mario Lemieux, what would you say . . . if God put anybody on this earth to do one particular thing, it's Mario Lemieux to play hockey. He had that stride . . . he had the ugliest, heavy stick—so heavy—but, man, he could do magic with that stick. Absolute friggin' magic. Incredible."

Thirty-some-odd years after his first hockey card was jammed into wax packs, Ruskowski is still in the game. He started his head coaching career in the WHL in 1989–90 and, with the exception of a couple of seasons, he has been behind the bench ever since. His hockey adventure, at least according to those who keep track of it with little pieces of cardboard, began with his first picture on that great "disco" card at the Aeros' old practice facility.

"I was living the life. I was playing with Gordie Howe, in a warm climate. You could play golf in the afternoon." And at night, of course, you'd hit the town. "I used to go to discos with my roommate and my linemates at night. Oh yeah, chains, big [platform shoes]. I love the high heels cause I'm only 5-foot-9."

As for the anti-aging thing, it came to a screeching halt after his double exposure in '79–80.

"I got the wrinkles now, my friend. [When] I look back, I [see I] didn't have much talent but I was sure blessed. I had the opportunity to play with some great, great players. Stan Mikita, Lemieux, Howe, Marcel Dionne. I am truly blessed. Truly, truly blessed."

Don CHERRY 1974–75 OPC #161

No one tells Don Cherry how to dress. Well, okay, maybe *someone* does.

The man known as Grapes, who is beamed into television sets across Canada every Saturday night during the NHL season, can tell you exactly where he was when this fine photo was taken.

On June 13, 1974, the Boston Bruins held a press conference to announce that one Donald S. Cherry was the new head coach of Bobby Orr and the Bruins.

"It was a funny thing, Dick Williams was there. Remember Dick Williams the baseball guy? If ya took a picture of us, we looked alike. We both had the same mustache and the whole deal. So I always remember that as I had a nice blue suit on." Yes, the blue suit went well with the 'stache. If you're wondering about the 'stache, it didn't last as long as the suit did.

"I had it for about two months and then I shaved it off. For luck," says Cherry.

When it came to facial hair, Cherry could call his own shots. And as any living, breathing hockey fan knows, when it comes to style, Cherry also calls his own shots. Well, except when it came to his '74–75 O-Pee-Chee; take a close look at the card—Cherry is dapper as always.

"It was a dark blue [suit] with a vest, and I wore a nice chain with it. The whole deal. So I looked pretty sharp."

The hair is well groomed, as always. But as far as Cherry is concerned, one thing is not right on this card. It's the tie. The tie still bothers Cherry after all these years. And it's a double whammy.

Issue number one, the knot. "I cannot believe I had a knot that big in the tie!" But responsibility for the knot is all on Cherry. Let's face it; big knots were in at the time.

It's issue number two that's the real kicker. Don Cherry says his tie was airbrushed. Imagine airbrushing a man who used ZZ Top's "Sharp Dressed Man" for his theme song when he hosted *Grapevine*? Cherry insists that's what happened.

Nobody tells Don Cherry how to dress. "That's right," he says.

But the card makers did. When Don Cherry was introduced as the new head coach of the Boston Bruins, he says he showed up in a slick blue suit with a sharp blue tie. But that's not how he is remembered on his '74–75 OPC.

"One thing I remember when I look at the picture is that actually it was a blue tie. They painted a red tie, right? They changed it to the red tie," says Cherry, who went on to coach 400 regular season games with the Bruins.

You can't tell him how to dress, but you can change his clothes after the fact. But few can tell him what to say, and as Cherry recalls this card, he also recalls the press conference. As per usual, when he was on the mic, he rocked it from the start.

"You're kind of nervous in the front of the Boston press and all that. And I remember the guy saying, 'Do you think you're ready for the Boston Bruins?' and I said, 'The question is, are the Boston Bruins ready for me?'" chuckles Cherry.

His relationship with the media in a different era is what comes to mind with this card. There were no 24-hour sports networks, no instant news via Twitter and the internet. It truly was a different time.

"That day I was hired I remember how good the Boston press was to a minor-leaguer," says Cherry, who was 40 years old the day the Bruins made him their head man. "They knew I was going to be good press for them. Somehow the writers and that know who's going to be good when you go to a press conference, who's going to be good material for them. And I remember they were kind to me right off the bat. And we kind of faltered in that first year and they still didn't give it to me. That was the thing I remember."

When Don Cherry was behind the Boston bench, he was in charge of Bobby Orr, Phil Esposito, Wayne Cashman and a slew of other stars. Not bad for a guy who just a few years earlier was out of the game, looking for work. "I had no job or anything. And in three years I was coaching Bobby Orr. So I was always thank the Lord on that one."

How life changed for Don Cherry that day is hard to describe. No, he never led the Bruins to a Stanley Cup, but what a time he had. Looking back now, he figures he'd change a few things.

"When I look at that card, I think, 'You should have taken charge right off the bat.'"

But Cherry and his troops did bring one rough, tough style to the old Boston Garden. And the Bruins were good. Cherry took the Bruins to the Stanley Cup Final twice during his five years in Boston. Cherry won the Jack Adams in 1975–76 as NHL's coach of the year.

The rest, as they say, is history, and it's his history and his old Bruins team that come to mind whenever Don Cherry sees this card. That, and the fact that someone changed the colour of his tie.

"The only thing I can think of when I look at that picture, to tell you the truth, is I look at that bloody tie . . . and they airbrushed it," says Cherry, before conceding one final point. "Ya know, to tell you the truth, it looks better red. I have to admit."

Glenn Goldup 1974–75 OPC #275

"Fu Manchu, baby!" Those are the first words Glenn Goldup shouts out when the topic of this sweet '74–75 card comes up. That and the fact that the card makers spelled his name wrong on the front of the card; there are supposed to be two Ns in Glenn.

"How about they spell my name one way on the front and another on the back, did you notice that?"

How about we focus on the look? Which is awesome and pure mid-'70s Doobie Brothers. As for sitting down and striking that pose, Goldup does not remember the moment. "Can I take you back to that day? Shit, I can't remember when I took my last dump for crying out loud."

But Goldup does remember when he decided to go with the Doobie Brothers look, and where he got his inspiration. And it wasn't from the band. "[The look] started in Junior. At that time, long hair was in and I, at a young age, started a moustache and then I think I saw a hockey card of somebody who had this long Fu Manchu moustache and I thought, 'I'm going to try that.'" He tried it and it worked.

"Somebody said, 'Man, does that ever make you look mean.' And I said, 'Maybe I should just keep this look going then. You know, get this mean look going. People look at me sideways.' I think it's just the way that I looked at myself. I knew I wasn't a pretty boy."

Goldup struck this pose sometime during the '73–74 season, likely not all that long after Montreal took him with the 17th pick in the 1973 draft. Goldup met Habs coach Scotty Bowman at the Royal York Hotel in Toronto to sign his first contract. And just like he was on the card, Goldup was very fashionable that day as well.

"I came into the Royal York Hotel to do our deal and I walked in with a big gaucho hat—a big brown hat—and a full-length leather coat. I was styling. But I've always been that way. I dress that way still."

Goldup and his Fu Manchu were then off to Montreal. He got this card after suiting up in only six games during his rookie season. Getting a card that early was pretty rare back in the day. Goldup spent the next few years trying to crack the Habs full time, trying to make an impression on the legendary Scotty Bowman.

"Scotty was a genius at keeping you off guard," says Goldup. "I'll give you an example of it. I was playing on a line with Yvon Lambert and Peter Mahovlich. We played about three or four, five games together, and we were producing some pretty good results. I think I only got one assist out of all those games with limited ice time, because if they killed penalties and stuff I'd sit."

One day Goldup picked up the paper. In it Bowman was praising the efforts of young Goldup. "He said, 'I don't know what makes them work but the chemistry's working. That line's playing really well. Goldup's really filling in.' The whole bit. So that morning, I come walking to the dressing room. I'm walking down the hallway and he's walking towards me from the other end of the hallway. And I'm thinking about what he said in the paper and I'm smiling, and he walked right by me like he didn't even know I was there. And then, you just know, I'm walking into the dressing room and I'm going 'What the fuck?'—you know what I mean?"

On another occasion, the reason for Bowman's dismay with Goldup was a lot more obvious. Let's face it: Montreal is one fun town. One can only imagine what it was like for a young member of the Montreal Canadiens in the mid-'70s. One night, Goldup and his pal Rick Chartraw were enjoying the perks of Montreal nightlife. The exploits of the night caught up to them the next morning, when Chartraw and Goldup found themselves running late for practice.

"We were partying our asses off. It was a practice where we had to get dressed at the Forum and we practiced in Verdun. So we get in the car, and we know we're screwed. So we get to the Forum and we get in our gear, get in the car, drive to Verdun. First thing Scotty Bowman does, he says, 'You get in that room, and you get in *that* room!' So he separated us right away."

There should not have been a problem. On their way to Verdun,

Goldup and Chartraw had come up with perfect excuses for their tardiness: they stayed up late painting an apartment? Or was it that their car broke down? I smell trouble.

"I said the car wouldn't start and he said we were painting the apartment late and we got up late. The thing was Charty and I had said to each other, you know what, here's what we're going to say. But by the time we got out there, we forgot what we were going to say."

Eventually the would-be painter and mechanic made their way out onto the ice. Bowman got down to business. He sent Goldup and Chartraw to one end of the ice. Their teammates got to watch it all. "We were doing these drills and you got to have the pucks and you're skating around in one end zone. And Scotty would point in one direction and you'd have to go that way, and he'd point in another direction and you'd have to go that way. And he had us doing it with all the rest of the team watching. And we ran into each other," Goldup says, while trying to control his laughter. "Needless to say, about a week later I was back in Halifax."

Glenn Goldup played in 18 games over three seasons for the Montreal Canadiens before he was traded to the L.A. Kings. To this day, Goldup, who lives in Toronto, still roots for the Canadiens. He still gets that feeling of Habs magic when he looks at this old card.

"It's a very proud moment. It's a hugely proud moment and one that I'll always be proud of. Even today I'm a Montreal Canadiens fan. I'm a Habs fan. It makes people in Toronto crazy. They say, 'You live in Toronto,' but I say, 'You have to realize the Montreal Canadiens picked me! The Toronto Maple Leafs didn't—the Montreal Canadiens did.'

"It was the greatest experience of my life. The French culture and the French chemistry in the room was unbelievable. It was so much fun. In that room, the players were tight and there was no animosity towards French, English or anything else."

"I've always missed something since I stopped playing and I always will. It's not about the NHL or anything else. It's just about the game of hockey. The game of hockey was so much fun for me. I remember myself giggling and smiling while I was playing. I guess I'll always, forever, miss playing the game."

And Goldup misses that old look too. He's in sales now, but if he wasn't, the long locks and the Fu Manchu might still be around.

"When I got into business, I had to look a little more professional. Otherwise I'd still have long hair hanging down to my ass."

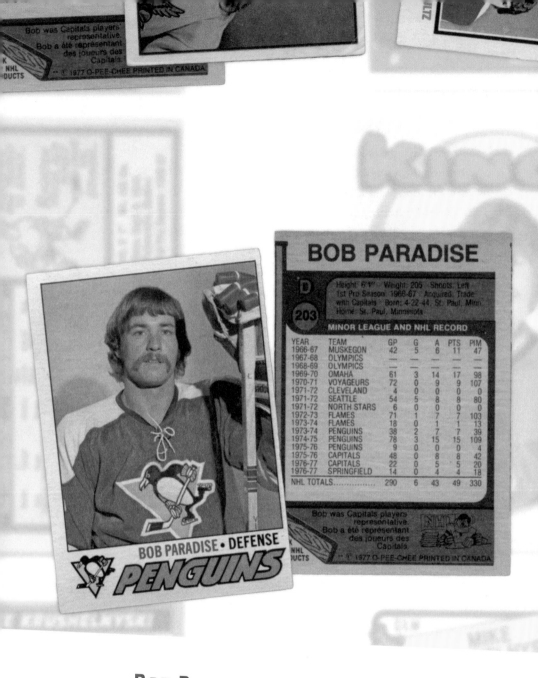

BOB PARADISE

D	Height: 6'1" Weight: 205 Shoots: Left 1st Pro Season: 1966-67 Acquired: Trade with Capitals Born: 4-22-44, St. Paul, Minn. Home: St. Paul, Minnesota	
203		

MINOR LEAGUE AND NHL RECORD

YEAR	TEAM	GP	G	A	PTS	PIM
1966-67	MUSKEGON	42	5	6	11	47
1967-68	OLYMPICS	—	—	—	—	—
1968-69	OLYMPICS	—	—	—	—	—
1969-70	OMAHA	61	3	14	17	98
1970-71	VOYAGEURS	72	0	9	9	107
1971-72	CLEVELAND	4	0	0	0	0
1971-72	SEATTLE	54	5	8	8	80
1971-72	NORTH STARS	6	0	0	0	0
1972-73	FLAMES	71	1	7	7	103
1973-74	FLAMES	18	0	1	1	13
1973-74	PENGUINS	38	2	7	7	39
1974-75	PENGUINS	78	3	15	15	109
1975-76	PENGUINS	9	0	0	0	4
1975-76	CAPITALS	48	0	8	8	42
1976-77	CAPITALS	22	0	5	5	20
1976-77	SPRINGFIELD	14	0	4	4	18
NHL TOTALS		290	6	43	49	330

Bob was Capitals players'
representative.
Bob a été représentant
des joueurs des
Capitals.

© 1977 O-PEE-CHEE PRINTED IN CANADA

BOB PARADISE • DEFENSE

PENGUINS

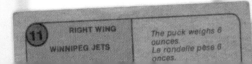

BOB PARADISE 1977–78 OPC #203

Awesomeness. Pure awesomeness. This picture was so nice that O-Pee-Chee used it twice. That's something Bob Paradise was not aware of at all.

A card maker using the same picture on more than one card wasn't overly rare in the 1970s. But on this occasion it at least made sense. On October 1, 1977, the Washington Capitals shipped Bob Paradise to the Pittsburgh Penguins for the rights to Don Awrey. Instead of going with a nasty airbrush job, or "now with Pittsburgh" typed across the front of the card, the card makers just went with the same photo they'd used for Paradise's 1975–76 card.

This is not a big deal to Bob Paradise. "I didn't have the cards until years after I was done. People started sending them for autographs. There was no market for that stuff."

And when you talk to Bob Paradise, you realize why being on a hockey card was not a big deal to him. This may sound a little strange, but even the fact that he made it to the NHL wasn't really that big of a deal for the native of St. Paul, Minnesota. He played hockey because he enjoyed the game. He graduated from St. Mary's College in Minnesota in 1966, not exactly a hockey hotbed at the time. In fact, Bob could have tried for a pro baseball career but chose to play college hockey instead. "I just liked hockey and didn't think I wanted to be a baseball player. And there was no money in it so I just stayed in school."

Once he graduated, the hockey world came calling. "I graduated in 1966. I was put on a C form by Montreal after my senior year, which meant they paid me a hundred bucks [and] if I ever signed—they owned me. That's what a C form was in 1966. And since I hadn't planned on playing, I thought I just made a hundred bucks. It was beautiful."

For the next two years, he played some minor pro and with the U.S. Olympic team and taught ninth and tenth grade English. A life in the NHL never occurred to him. Then one night he checked out a Minnesota North Stars game.

"I saw that they had all these old guys coming out of retirement to staff these teams. So I said, 'I may as well go to training camp.' I decided

I wasn't going to be a teacher forever. And I spent a couple years in the minor leagues and then I made it."

Bob Paradise says this without the slightest hint of bragging. He simply states it. To Bob, being a teacher and then making it to the NHL was no big deal. If something like this happened today, it would be on the cover of every major hockey publication and lead every sports highlight show on the planet. To make it even better, Bob made the NHL with his hometown Minnesota North Stars. Again, no big deal.

"We didn't think much of it. It wasn't a big deal. I mean, I was happy to do it, had a great time. Loved it, but there was no emphasis . . . I mean, you made it or you didn't. You went home and you got a job. That's what everybody did. That's what all the kids around Canada did. It was a much different story when kids started making money and then the media is all over every step they take from that day forth."

So that is why having a hockey card with his picture on it is not a big deal to Bob Paradise. He is quick to point out a couple of things about this card though. First up, his awesome '70s look—the 'stache and the hair. "That was in style at the time. I didn't make it up." Is his 'stache still around? The answer is no. "I'm all cleaned up now."

As for the sweet light blue Pens colours, maybe they weren't a big deal at the time, but looking back, they are on the cool side. "It was a mean-looking penguin compared to the passive one they have now on their shirt. The old penguin was cool.

"There wasn't that much, what do you call it, *fashion* involved in sport at the time. Whatever shirt they gave you and whatever colour it was, it was fine to everybody. Now they change them every two months. You know you've got a new shirt. But I liked the old stuff. I thought it was good. I like the new stuff too. I like the black and gold of Pittsburgh."

And even though his cards are not a big deal to him, it turns out they are to a few members of his family. "I'm proud of it and I have grandkids that are crazy over it and think I'm the best. Better than Crosby, and it's fun for them. I just feel fortunate to have had a chance to play."

164 1979-80 NHL PENALTY MINUTE LDRS / JOUEURS LES PLUS PÉNALISÉS

Player - Joueur - Team - Équipe	Minutes
Jimmy Mann, Winnipeg	287
Dave Williams, Toronto/Vancouver	278
Paul Holmgren, Philadelphia	267
Terry O'Reilly, Boston	265
Terry Ruskowski, Chicago	252
Paul Mulvey, Washington	240
Willi Plett, Atlanta	231
Garry Howatt, N.Y. Isl.	219
	212
	208

© NHLPA 1980
PRINTED IN CANADA

O-PEE-CHEE 1979-80 NHL PENALTY MINUTE LEADERS / JOUEURS LES PLUS PÉNALISÉS

1 **JIMMY MANN** JETS 2 **DAVE WILLIAMS** CANUCKS 3 **PAUL HOLMGREN** FLYERS

JIMMY MANN 1980–81 OPC #164
PENALTY MINUTES LEADERS

If you were going to be on a hockey card, why wouldn't you look happy about it? Jimmy Mann may hold the distinction of being the happiest-looking guy to ever grace a Penalty Minutes Leaders card.

"It was one of those pictures, you don't realize the topic until you get to the end of the year . . . I was like that

MAKING IT LOOK MEAN

anyway. I smiled all the time."

The picture was taken before Mann knew he was going to burst onto the NHL scene and lead the league in penalty minutes during his rookie season. If he knew that, maybe he would have tried to look a little meaner, like the other two guys on the card: the legendary Tiger Williams and the Flyers' Paul Holmgren.

"You look at Holmgren, you look at Tiger; Tiger never smiles anyway, and Paul Holmgren—you know, he doesn't smile very much either. They were pretty tough players."

The reason Mann can't stop smiling on this card is the same reason he didn't stop smiling for much of the 1979–80 season; he made the NHL straight out of the Quebec Major Junior Hockey League at the tender age of 20. "I was smiling because I was playing in the National Hockey League."

The whole experience was almost unbelievable to Jimmy Mann. Just a few weeks before making the Jets, Mann was drafted by Winnipeg as the 19th overall pick in 1979. Back in those days, players didn't attend the draft.

When Mann got a phone call on draft day, he wasn't buying what he was being told.

"I got a call from someone who said, 'Jimmy, you're drafted in the first round.' I thought it was one of my friends. I told him, 'Yeah, right, sure,' but it was a journalist from somewhere."

Mann brought his tough brand of hockey to the Jets. He put up some great offensive numbers in Junior. In his final season with the Sherbrooke Castors, Mann scored 35 goals and added 47 assists for 82 points in 65 games. He also racked up 260 PIMS. Like any smart hockey player, when he got to Winnipeg, he quickly figured out what he'd have to do to stick in the Big Leagues.

"[The Jets] didn't have a tough team then. They had lost all their players after the World Hockey [draft] so there weren't very many tough players. We had Dave Hoyda, he was sort of a little bit on his way out . . . and there was myself, at 20. That's the way it was and I was going to do what I could to stay there."

If you're going to try and do the tough-guy thing, why not dive right in? The Winnipeg Jets hosted the Boston Bruins in late October during Mann's rookie season. The Bruins had a loaded and lethal lineup. Three of their toughest players were Terry O'Reilly, Al Secord and Stan Jonathan. Dropping the gloves with one of those guys on any given night would have been an accomplishment. On that night though, Jimmy Mann danced with all three.

"I fought O'Reilly, Jonathan and Secord. Three fights in three shifts. I did really, really well. [Mike] Milbury, I knocked the crap out of him in the corner and then I fought O'Reilly, which was a good fight and I gave him a pretty good shot. Secord too, I got a picture of it, and Jonathan. I was 20 years old so I was making a name pretty early there, you know. But it was exciting, and it was exciting to be in the National Hockey League and I owe everything to Fergie [John Ferguson] for drafting me and giving me that opportunity."

With a pace like that, it's no wonder that Mann ended up leading the

NHL with 287 PIMS in his rookie season. Flip the card over and look at the rest of the PIM leaders; two of the three Bruins Mann dropped the gloves with that October night, O'Reilly and Jonathan, are in the top ten, so it's safe to say Mann wasn't side-stepping anyone.

This card is one of the few out there of Jimmy Mann. He played in the NHL until the '87–88 season. He wasn't always up in the Big Leagues for the final few years of his career, but he says that's not why he stopped showing up on hockey cards. He has his own theory as to why he only had three cards. His last one was issued in the 1981–82 set.

"My second year is when I hit Paul Gardner."

It was a brutal hit. It was the kind of hit that affects two careers. Gardner had just cross-checked Mann's teammate Doug Smail in the face. As things were settling down, Mann came from out of nowhere and blindsided the Pittsburgh Penguins forward with a vicious left to the face. Gardner's jaw broke in two places. Mann got a 10-game suspension and ended up in Manitoba court on assault charges. He received a suspended sentence and was fined $500. Gardner's lawyer was Alan Eagleson, who was also the head of the National Hockey League Players' Association.

"[Eagleson] blackballed me for the rest of my career with cards. After that hit, I never had a card. He blackballed me because I broke [Gardner's] jaw and finished his career, and [Eagleson] never put my name in for another card again.

"Every player got one every year. I went to his right-hand man then, and I said, 'What the fuck? What's going on with no cards?' 'Well, we sent your pictures in.' I said, 'Yeah, like fuck you did.' But I never got another card from the NHL after that.

"I was a little pissed off I didn't get any more. But what are you going to do? It wasn't all that important then, but it's always fun to have cards. I got my rookie card, I got my penalty minutes one, and I got another one my second year."

And that was it for Mann's hockey-card run. Like most other players of days gone by, he has been featured in a number of nostalgia sets over the years, but he still remembers the first time he saw that old Penalty Minutes Leaders card.

"I saw it the first year. I said, 'Ah, shit.' It was pretty cool. It was probably the only award, the only thing I ever won anyway, that year or any year."

These days Jimmy Mann is a regular on the NHL old-timer's circuit. He's reached a whole new generation of fans that never saw him suit up in an NHL game. He sees his cards all the time, his rookie card, his PIMs card and his second-year card, which turned out to be the final card of his NHL career. He wouldn't mind, though, if he had the chance to see a few more. "It would have been nice to have another five or six of them."

PHIL ROBERTO 1973–74 OPC #3

My brother, Peter, and I had it good when we were growing up on Grange Street in Pictou, Nova Scotia. We had a big yard and a spotlight on our driveway where we would play road hockey all night with our buddies Craig and Randy. Actually we wouldn't play all night; the game would usually end in a fight, almost always someone versus Randy. I'm not sure why he was involved in so many scraps.

Peter and I shared a gigantic bedroom. It was a sports card geek's dream. We set up displays all over the place.

My brother, who was by far the better, more skilled hockey player, seemed to have an affinity for the game's darker side. He had a display over his bed that was pretty basic: a piece of paper with a few cards taped on it, and "Goons of the Game" written in Pete's trusty handwriting above the seven or eight cards.

Of course, there were the usual suspects (you know the names), but there was one card in Pete's display that stood out. A 1973–74 card of a player named Phil Roberto. We didn't really know who Phil Roberto was—we knew that he wasn't a goon but we also knew that this card had to be a part of the display.

We had never seen anything like it. The card showed a raging mad Roberto, his right fist ready to deliver a blow to his opponent as a referee tried to bust things up. For years Peter and I marvelled at this card. Who was this guy? What was the deal with this card? A fight on a hockey card, really?

The phone rang one morning after a late night shift at Sportsnet. On the other end was the one and only Phil Roberto. Kind enough to return the message I had left him, he was on the line from Alabama where he now lives.

"I used to be a guy who loved to be around the net, and Billy Smith, as you know, was pretty good at clearing out his net with his stick. And if I recall correctly he struck me, so I went at him," says Roberto.

Finally, an explanation.

"The game now is goalies are pretty much taboo . . . you can go in their areas but you can't mess with them," says Roberto. "I think the players still protect their goaltenders. Now you see a lot of scrums, now it's totally, mostly face washing."

A quick look at the back of Roberto's card shows you he's no goon. He did not spend a ton of time in the box. A solid 99 PIMs in that '72–73 season, the year he dropped the gloves with Billy Smith.

And that's the other cool thing about this card: Roberto is fighting No. 31 of the New York Islanders. That's the great Billy Smith! Hey, if you're going to pick a 'tender to have a go with, it might as well be one of, if not the, toughest ever. "Billy was a total competitor. You didn't go around his net. If you did, you were going to get spanked."

Roberto, it seems, had a thing for goalies though, and making his way into the crease. "My game was, I liked to play physical and give it my all when I was out there and if it took going through the crease or whatever, I did that."

Once upon a time that style ticked off another Hall of Fame goaltender. This time Roberto did not have to drop the gloves and the incident in question did not end up on a hockey card. But the incident did have a second Hall of Fame connection.

"Another goalie that didn't really like me was Gerry Cheevers. I was in Boston and he chased me. He was coming at me one night out of his net. Beliveau got the puck because Cheevers was chasing me and put it in the net."

That's Beliveau as in Jean. Before arriving in St. Louis, Roberto played for the Montreal Canadiens. He won a Cup with the Habs and had a couple of other thrills as well, both courtesy of Jean Beliveau.

"I assisted on his 500th goal and I think I scored on his 600th assist or something like that, which was another highlight of my career."

But it was in St. Louis where Roberto came out of his hockey shell. He had a magical playoff run in the spring of 1972. It was one of those come-from-nowhere, light-the-lamp kind of playoffs you see every couple of years from an unsung hero. Roberto scored seven goals and added six assists for 13 points in 11 games before the Boston Bruins swept the Blues in the second round.

"I don't think I got hot at the right time. I was just playing my game the way I always played it," says Roberto. "I was just, I'd say, an average hard-working player. You know there were so many superstars in Montreal. You saw no power-play time or anything like that because the depth there with the players was just phenomenal. So I got a lot more ice time when I played in St. Louis."

That ice time ultimately produced one dandy hockey card. Roberto can't really recall seeing the card during his playing days; it popped up years later. "I think that was the last fighting card ever made, from what I hear," says the man who picked up 181 career points in 385 NHL games.

If you see another fighting card let Phil Roberto know, and if you happen to run into the goalie on Phil's 1973–74 card . . . "Say hi to Billy for me."

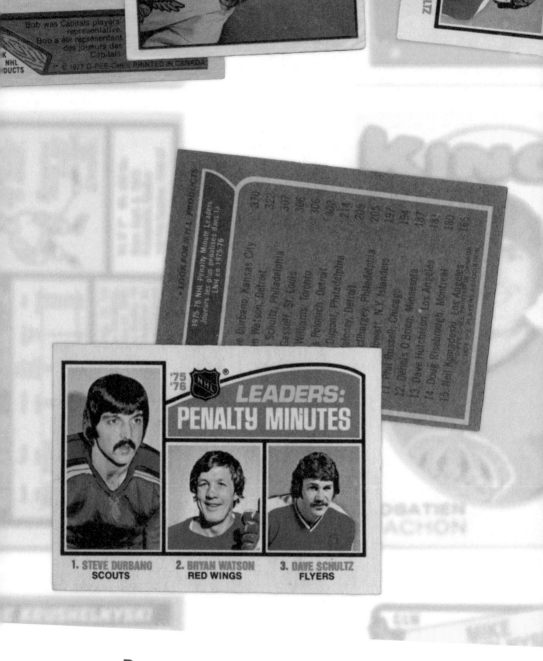

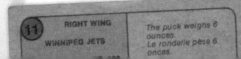

Bryan Watson
PENALTY MINUTES LEADERS 1976–77 OPC #4

In terms of tough guy hockey cards, this could be one of the best of all time. The colours are awesome, the design is simple and the top penalty minutes leaders from the 1975–76 season are all legends.

Leading the way with 370 penalty minutes, in a sweet airbrushed uniform, is one of the most notorious men to ever skate in the National Hockey League, the late Steve Durbano. This guy was straight out of *Slap Shot*. Once upon a time he ripped the hair—the wig—right off Bobby Hull's head during a WHA melee.

At number three, the Muscle on Broad Street: Dave Schultz, clocking in at 307 penalty minutes.

And at number two, a man who spanned two generations of hockey, Detroit's Bryan Watson. He crossed the finish line with 322 penalty minutes in '75–76.

Pro hockey was going through a transition in the mid-'70s. To put it bluntly, NHL teams were engaged in an arms race. Teams didn't have one tough guy. They had three, four or maybe even five, and the guys on this card were leading the way. They had a strong supporting cast too. Turn this card over and take a look at the names that finished behind this trio in the PIMS race: Gassoff, Williams, Polonich, Dupont and Howatt, to name a few.

So let's talk about this card, the men on it and the wild times of the mid-'70s.

"It's 90 degrees outside in Washington, this time last week it was 30, and I get a call about Durbano and Schultz," says Bryan Watson from his pizza shop just outside of Washington, D.C. "It's just funny, you know? I did a thing on the weekend for cancer. I did a card signing, a charity thing, and I actually saw that card a few times. It's a great card."

Do some quick math. Durbano, Watson and Schultz combined to get 999 penalty minutes in 1975–76. That's 16 hours and 39 minutes in the box.

"It makes me laugh. [The card] brought back memories, not knowing when we were being wild and crazy and young guys that they'd actually have a card with three of us on it," says Watson, who according to HockeyFights.com dropped the gloves 14 times during the '75–76 season. During that season he never dropped the gloves with either Schultz or Durbano, but they did have their run-ins over the years.

Durbano is legendary among hockey fight connoisseurs. A look at his career stats gives you a glimpse into how he played the game. He wasn't a goal scorer. He wasn't a playmaker. During hockey's bloodiest era, Durbano was muscle. In 220 career NHL games, he sat in the box for 1,127 minutes. He played another 45 games in the WHA and racked up 284 PIMS.

"He always pushed the envelope," Watson says of the 6-foot-1, 210-pound Durbano. "He wasn't that tough at all. He was just wild and crazy. But as far as toughness, a guy like John Ferguson would chew him up and spit him out."

"I fought with [Durbano] and he was a hell of a lot bigger than me," Watson says. Durbano had trouble with the law after his pro hockey career, spending time in prison. For a long time, he was as wild off the ice as he was on it. He had some crazy moments on the ice that are now just a click away on YouTube. Type in the name Durbano, and it is all there: an epic brawl against Ranger Nick Fotiu, an attack on Bobby Hull and a brawl with Kevin Morrison.

"He was over the edge, that's his own deal. I mean that's how he got [to pro hockey] and that's how he stayed there, kept a job—and more power to him."

Look at the right-hand corner on this card, and another legend appears, Dave "The Hammer" Schultz. His grin almost seems to say, "Go ahead, go for it. I'm ready."

The Flyers were stacked with talent. They had Bobby Clarke, Bill Barber, Reggie Leach and Bernie Parent. And they had the Hammer.

"He couldn't have planned it better. He was in the right place at the right time," says Watson. "[Schultz] was the final piece of the puzzle that made [the Flyers a championship team]. They went from being bullies to the Broad Street Bullies. And we're like all tough guys: you love them when they're on your team and hate them when you play against them. But I respected [Schultz] for what he did and as long as he lasted. It was fabulous.

"He and I had some altercations, but I think a lot of guys who were in the situation we were all in, we respected each other. It wasn't like they had to beat me or I had to beat him to beat Philly."

The one thing this card does not reveal is just how unreal it was for Bryan Watson to appear on it in the first place. Durbano and Schultz were, for the most part, young whippersnappers. In '75–76 Durbano was 24 years old; Dave Schultz was 26. Bryan Watson was 33, not old by any means, but in the mid-'70s it wasn't exactly young for an NHLer. Luckily Watson had plenty of muscle with him on the Wings.

"In Detroit we had a hell of a tough team, with Maloney and Hextall and Polonich. We had some tough kids; we weren't intimidated by Philly at all. What happened was after the first shift Schultz would get kicked out and then we had to play hockey. And that's when we were in trouble."

Schultz and Durbano were part of the Expansion Era, as was Watson. But Watson was also part of the Original Six. "I played when there were only six teams in the world. Which is pretty special." One of Watson's teammates while he was breaking into the pro game was the legendary Doug Harvey. It was Defence 101 for the younger player. "He was the smartest guy I ever played with. The smartest man I ever knew. Hockey wise, his knowledge of the game was unbelievable. And of course he was Bobby Orr before Bobby Orr. He was the reason the Montreal Canadiens were a great team. He was the fourth forward. Along with being one of the most generous and kind people I've ever met, he was really, really intelligent about the game and really competitive. Tremendous ability. My God, when I played with him he was an old man and he could still pass the puck better than most of the guys in the National Hockey League."

When Watson finished his pro career after splitting the '78–79 season with Washington and the WHA's Cincinnati Stingers, he was, by hockey standards, an old man of 36. Watson played in 878 NHL regular season games. His final stat line reads 17 goals, 135 assists, 152 points and 2,212 penalty minutes. A career-high 322 PIMS came in '75–76 and got him a spot on this outstanding piece of cardboard.

1981-82 NHL Penalty Minute Leaders
Joueurs les plus pénalisés
dans la LNH en 1981-82

	Team / Équipe	Min Min
	Pittsburgh Penguins	407
	Vancouver Canucks	341
	Philadelphia Flyers	329
	Pittsburgh Penguins	322
	Chicago Black Hawks	303
	Calgary Flames	288
	Philadelphia Flyers	275
Dale Hunter	Quebec Nordiques	272
Bob McGill	Toronto Maple Leafs	263
Randy Holt	Washington Capitals	259

©NHLPA 1982
©1982 O-Pee-Chee Ptd. in Canada-Imprimé au Canada

1981
1982

NHL

1981-82 NHL
Penalty Minute
Leader

Joueur le plus
pénalisé dans la
LNH en 1981-82

PAUL BAXTER

O-PEE-CHEE

PAUL BAXTER 1982–83 OPC #238
PENALTY MINUTES LEADERS

I'm not sure where I got this card. I must have ripped it out of a pack at a very young age, because it's always been around. Its first home, other than a wax pack, was likely my old hockey-skates card box.

I always liked tough guys; maybe that's why this card has always stood out to me. But who really cares what I think about it? Let's find out from Paul Baxter himself, who racked up an extremely impressive 409 penalty minutes in 1981–82. The card lists Baxter's PIM total at 407. But the number you will come up with on NHL.com and HockeyDb .com is 409. It's the second-highest single season total in NHL history.

The card, for the most part, is pretty ordinary. Maybe that's why it doesn't really stand out for Baxter. What does stand out for the player is a season where he racked up more than 400 minutes in the box.

"First of all we didn't have a very big team. Believe it or not, I played the power play, I played a lot of minutes. I guess I got into situations where I backed up a lot of teammates."

A quick look at Baxter's regular season stats makes you do a double take. He did rack up the points, an impressive 43, to go along with almost seven hours of penalties. Baxter dropped the gloves with the toughest and meanest men in the NHL: Tiger Williams, Chris Nilan, Nick Fotiu and Jimmy Mann all showed up on his dance card. So how did he manage to attract such a wide array of tough guys?

"I think I always played a pretty aggressive game and I was able to skate pretty well, and I think I initiated a lot of contact with some pretty hard open ice hits. Sometimes people didn't like that, and I've reflected on the other end where I thought a teammate was being taken advantage of. I guess it's kind of a collective effort I guess," laughs Baxter, who went on to a coaching career after his playing days. "I think when I played I was probably a little bit of a shit disturber. Probably. I think that would be safe to say."

One night in November 1981 at the old Montreal Forum, Baxter took his "disturbing" to a whole new level. His target was Montreal tough-guy Chris Nilan. Sadly, this story does not end up on the back of Baxter's PIM leader card, but it did help contribute to his penalty total. It all started when Nilan and Baxter collided along the boards.

"I really hit him hard and knocked him down," begins Baxter. Now if you need to know anything about Chris Nilan circa 1981 it was this: he was still trying to make a name for himself at the NHL level and he did not take any grief from anyone.

"I was already on the way back up ice and he came up from behind and I think I turned pretty quickly and my stick might have been up a little high and I might have caught him maybe in the face with a stick. Unintentional, of course," adds Baxter, with the slightest hint of sarcasm. "So we fought and came to the penalty box and he said something and I said something back to him that he clearly didn't like." Baxter can't remember what he specifically said to Nilan, but remember, Baxter is a self-admitted "disturber." Whatever Baxter said, it worked—Nilan became extremely disturbed.

"He picked up a puck out of the ice box in the penalty box area and threw it at me and cut me for three stitches on top of the head." Baxter was quickly escorted to the Forum's clinic.

"When I went to the Forum clinic, it was right between the two [dressing] rooms. So I walked in and laid down on the table and the doctor asked me to put my gloves and stick down and wait for the table. I had my stick in my hand and I took the gloves off, and I left the stick lying down beside me as he was stitching me, and sure enough Chris Nilan tried to get in the door!" Baxter is still quite amazed by this over 30 years later. However he feels as safe now as he did then; after all, he was a pretty tough guy, he was armed with his stick, plus he was behind security and one big door. "I think he got to the door and I think the security guards came in, but I thought I was pretty well protected."

So if you'd been wondering how Baxter ended up with 409 minutes in penalties in 1981–82, hopefully you have your answer now. And I, for one, understand why I've always been obsessed with this simple-looking hockey card. It turns out there is quite a story behind it.

OREST KINDRACHUK 1977–78 OPC #26

"They got a thousand pictures and they gotta use that one?"

That's Orest Kindrachuk's reaction when asked about this beauty. There are few cards like it. Kindrachuk's gloves are off, his jersey is in a frazzled state and there's blood under his left eye.

"I always say that blood was caused by a stick," says the 5-foot-10, 175-pound centre from the two-time Cup champion Broad Street Bullies. "I don't know if it was or not. You know what, I don't even remember who I fought in that game. For some reason I think it was against the Islanders. But as far as who I got in a fight with, I'm not sure I remember."

A little detective work reveals that Kindrachuk was in five scraps during the '76–77 season. Sure enough, one of them was against the Islanders' André St. Laurent on Long Island.

"You know what, I think it was St. Laurent. He and I didn't like each other," recalls Kindrachuk. "On the ice there were players that I just hated . . . Win at all costs. Sorry, this is a living. This isn't amateur. This is a living. You come into my house, you're taking my mortgage."

That attitude stayed with Kindrachuk during his entire 508 game NHL career. And it made for one fine specimen of a hockey card. Aside from his rough attitude, the card also shows off his splendid '70s look.

"Back then everybody looked like a porn star. I mean, not just our team but take a look at the pictures back then: long hair, moustache, the whole bit."

Kindrachuk famously revived his '70s look at the 2012 Winter Classic. These days he is clean-shaven and has far less hair compared to back then. At the Winter Classic, Kindrachuk decided to give his old teammates, opponents and the Citizens Bank Park fans the *Back to the Future* treatment" during the alumni game. His plan was to take to the ice looking like his 1970s self. All he needed to find was some hair and a moustache.

"My kids thought I was nuts; they came in for the game. They said, 'Dad, you're gonna really do that?' I said, 'Why not?'" Then Kindrachuk delivers a classic line: "You know it's not easy finding a wig. I'm not going to go spend 400 dollars on a wig for a gag." Thankfully, there was no need to fork over that kind of cash. "I went into this store. I said to the guy this is what I need and he said I got something for ya. It was perfect; it was 20 bucks.

"We were all getting ready to line up to go in to get introduced and I went into the can and put everything on and came walking out and it was pretty awesome."

The gag was priceless. Kindrachuk exited his impromptu change room looking like a 1977 version of himself. The long hair and the beauty moustache worked oh-so-well. For some folks, it was a convincing look. "There are people that actually thought that was still my hair." For the record, the hair for the moustache was trimmed off the wig and stuck on to Kindrachuk's upper lip with double-sided tape.

"I was facing off against [Mark] Messier and he said, 'That looked awesome.'"

The wig Kindrachuk sported on that January 2012 day in Philadelphia, just like the look on this card, recalls a magical time for the player: the days of the Broad Street Bullies, when the Flyers won two Cups in a row under the guidance of the legendary Fred Shero. Those were the days when Kindrachuk and the rest of the Flyers were Philadelphia royalty.

"In the '70s, especially the early to mid-'70s, this city with the Flyers was rocking. It was just a great era for hockey in Philadelphia. The people were behind this. They saw a bunch of Canadian kids on a blue-collar team that would win at all costs. And nobody, I don't believe, could ever out-work us. And I think that was what Philadelphia likes. It's a blue-collar town and, boy, at the time we fit right into that mold. Freddie Shero used to have us on the ice at nine o'clock in the morning. He says, 'You guys are going to work at nine just like everybody else.' Nowadays how many practices do they have at nine o'clock on the ice? At nine o'clock in the morning?"

What the Flyers did on the ice was legendary. What the fans did off the ice was legendary as well. HBO did a fantastic job telling the story of the Flyers with their documentary *Broad Street Bullies*. The Stanley Cup parade scenes are incredible: hundreds of thousands of people lining the streets of Philly. Kindrachuk loved the documentary, but he says HBO did skip over one part of the two parades that he will never forget.

"They didn't show any of the streakers," laughs Kindrachuk. Like the rest of the players, he rode in a car during the Flyers' first parade. After their second Cup win in '75, the Flyers got a much better view of the madness of the parade, and the streaking around them. The Flyers traded in cars for flatbed trucks.

"The second year we had a good view, we were up a little higher. I don't remember how many [streakers] there were, but then I don't think there was anything you could do wrong in Philadelphia, as a person at the parade or as a player. The city was crazy wild, but yet there was no damage, no looting, no anything. It was just a fun, wild parade."

Kindrachuk wasn't necessarily wild on the ice. His stats reveal he didn't fight much, but if you got in his way, it was go time, no matter who you were or what his odds were when he went up against you. "You do what you gotta do. You don't back down, I don't care who it is. I had a couple of fights with Terry O'Reilly and that was nuts because the first time I fought him I didn't know he was left handed." How long did it take Kindrachuk to realize he was up against a southpaw? "Immediately," he says.

"As a player you want to be remembered that you gave it your all every night and you could do whatever it takes to win. And if you do whatever it takes to succeed, good things will happen. Even if you don't win, good things will happen."

So, on second thought, for Kindrachuk, this '77–78 O-Pee-Chee card almost perfectly sums up his on-ice attitude and the Broad Street Bullies on-ice persona. "I start thinking 'Oh my God, haven't they got any better photographs?' But now that I look at it, you know what, I think that's what we were all about."

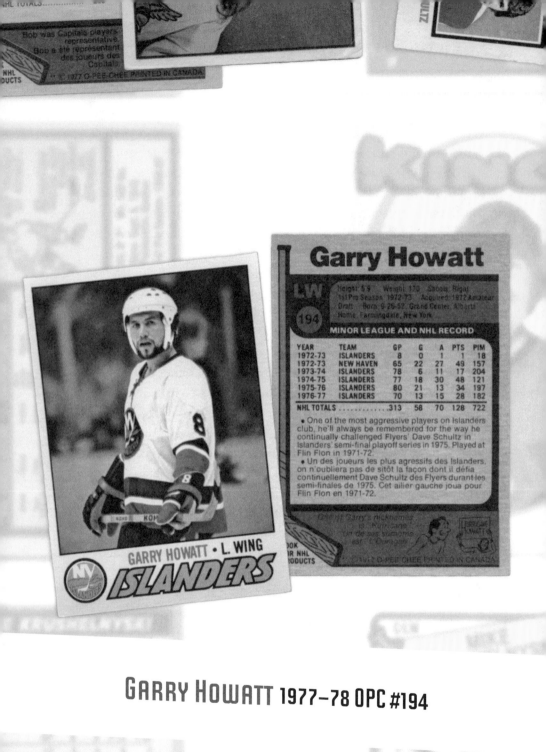

GARRY HOWATT 1977–78 OPC #194

Garry Howatt looks to be in a rather foul mood on his 1977–78 O-Pee-Chee and that makes sense. When it came to life on the ice, Howatt always played with an edge. Years later, if you think he's all sentimental when it comes to looking back at his hockey cards, you've got the wrong guy. "I don't know if I have a favourite," says Howatt.

So let's focus on his '77–78. Like most of his Islander teammates at the time, Howatt went with the classic Mikita or Potvin Northland helmet. He's not really sure why. For one thing, he didn't do it as a fashion statement.

"I have no idea why I friggin' went with that" is what Howatt offers. "I can't remember back that far. I'm old and I've had a few concussions, I think."

On the back of the card, it lists one of Howatt's nicknames as "The Hurricane," but most of the time he was known as "The Toy Tiger."

"Oh God. I had a bunch of different nicknames. I don't know how I got that. From the guys, I guess."

Toy Tiger is the one that stuck. Howatt's card lists him at 5-foot-9 and 170 pounds—not a giant by any means. But he played like a big man. And he danced with the biggest men the NHL had to offer. Through his first 313 NHL games, he racked up 722 penalty minutes.

A lot of guys who come up as goal scorers realize once they make the pros that there are a lot of goal scorers looking to make it to the NHL. So they change their roles. They becomes checkers, or in some cases tough guys. Garry Howatt was not one of those guys. He always played the game on the edge. He basically had no choice as he toughed it out on the ice as a teenager in northern Alberta. Sure he could score goals, but he could scrap as well. "I never took any crap. Where I come from [Glendon, now part of Cold Lake, Alberta], up there, you know if we didn't have a party at night and a fight, it was a bad weekend."

"When I was, like, 15 or 16, I was playing on a senior hockey team and when the first scout came up [to see me], I was in a fight with this

30-year-old guy when we were playing the air force team up in northern Alberta."

That statement leads to an obvious follow-up question. What was it like being a 15-year-old in a fight with a 30-year-old? Enjoy this classic Howatt answer: "I did that when I was 13," says Howatt. "[Fighting 30-year-olds] wasn't a big deal."

That explains the all-business look on his hockey card. It also fills you in on just how ready Howatt was to do anything to play in the NHL. A perfect example of that can be found in his bio on the back of the card: "He'll always be remembered for the way he continually challenged Flyers' Dave Schultz in Islanders' semi-final playoff series in 1975."

For the true story of the Toy Tiger versus the Hammer, you have to go back a few years to December 16, 1973, when Howatt and Schultz dropped the gloves for the first time in the NHL. According to HockeyFights.com, it was the first of nine fights they had against each other.

The much smaller Howatt, who gave up about a 35-pound weight advantage, is delivering rights to the hunched-over Schultz. Schultz is hunched over for a reason: Howatt's left hand has a clump of the Hammer's hair. Howatt delivers some right uppercuts that go unanswered before the refs break up the scrap. The play-by-play announcer sums up the scene perfectly: "Usually they're trying to save the little guy from the big guy."

That first Howatt-Schultz scrap was more than just your average tilt; it changed the game in regards to the rules of on-ice combat. "The next year they made that new rule: no hair pulling. I think he was knocked out on his feet there, then after that the next year they said, 'You can't pull hair.' Well, fuck me, we're in a fight for Chrissake. I nearly had my ear and nose bit off, you know, when we hit the ice. I thought you could do whatever you wanted in a fight."

It turns out you can't pull hair—at least not anymore. That makes things a lot more challenging when you're giving up at least 30 pounds and a few inches in most of your scraps. "When they're 6-foot-4 and 6-6, it was tough after that."

Howatt found a way to keep taking care of business though. Fast-forward to the 1975 Cup semifinal against Schultz and the Islanders. The Toy Tiger and Schultz fought four times in the series. A series the Broad Street Bullies eventually won in seven games, en route to their second straight Stanley Cup.

"Schultzie, he was a tough guy. There were a few [tough guys] there. There was no Dave Schultz on our team. We had a tough team you know, Clark Gillies and Bobby [Nystrom] and I. There's nobody tougher than those two guys," offers the modest Howatt.

All these years later, Howatt and the Hammer still meet on the ice. "We play charity games against them and stuff like that." They keep the gloves on. Howatt is quick to add that the Hammer and the rest of the Flyers are a bunch of great guys.

A couple of years after this card came out, Howatt's glare turned into a smile. He won two Stanley Cups with the Islanders in 1980 and 1981. A dispute over playing time prompted him to leave the Islanders for Hartford after the 1980–81 season. It's something that still upsets him.

"I didn't have to leave the Island. I just got upset I didn't play a couple series in the second Stanley Cup. I really kicked myself in the ass after that. My wife told me we should stay. You know, Al Arbour wanted me to stay for at least another year or two, but I was still young."

These days the Toy Tiger, who lives in Arizona, has mellowed, and he's still thrilled that he got to play in the NHL. "You couldn't beat it, all the kids dream of doing that. I mean, I would have been a farm boy or working on the oil rigs back home if I didn't make it. It was the best."

To Howatt, hockey cards are just evidence, a "been there, done that" kind of thing. "It just means I played in the NHL I guess. That's all it means."

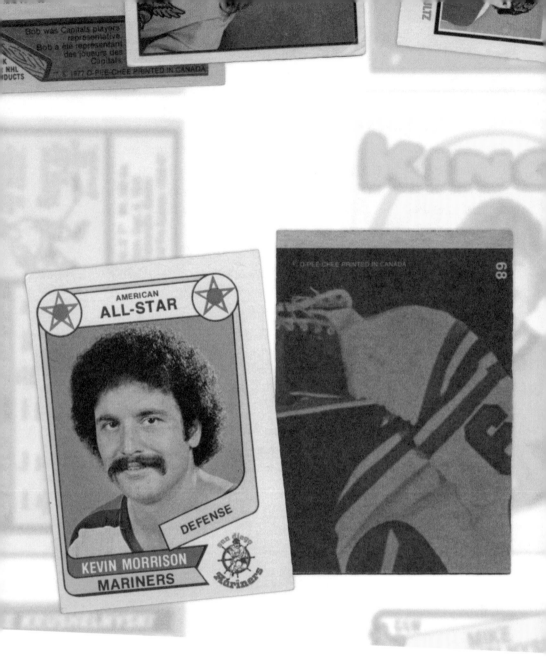

KEVIN MORRISON 1976–77 OPC #68 (WHA)

I grew up listening to my parents tell tales of all the great hockey players they knew from Cape Breton Island. They would list off the names: Junior Hanna, Paul Andrea, Kevin Morrison. It turns out they were all fantastic players. It also turns out that one day I would discover that Kevin Morrison had one of the coolest cards of all time. I'm not

Chapter Three — THE WHA

sure when I first stumbled on it, but wow, this card is awesome. It's a time machine on cardboard. There he is, a young 27-year-old Kevin Morrison. Smiling, styling, a WHA All-Star, top of the world, Ma!

"Everybody around town, they laugh when they see the picture, because now I got the grey hair and it's kind of laying flat on my head. It doesn't stand up anymore; it's too old. They can't believe that the hair and moustache was me," says Morrison.

Oh, but it was. The great thing about this pic of Morrison is that he got the double treatment from O-Pee-Chee. His All-Star card uses the same picture as his "normal" card, number 10 in the set. The fine folks at O-Pee-Chee just took a mid-'70s font, slapped "American All-Star" on it and an All-Star card was born. One picture, two cards.

Morrison remembers the day the picture was taken: no big whoop, good thing he just happened to be looking his best. "It was just a regular day after practice. I had to get prettied up to go out, you know."

And in the mid-1970s Kevin Morrison looked his best

pretty much all the time. The haircut came courtesy of a young lady who just happened to be at a Mariners game one night. Morrison already had the moustache, so why not add a little curl as well? Pre-permanent, Morrison offers up a '70s icon he resembled. Before you read on, take a look at the card one more time, picture flat hair, take a guess . . .

"The hair I had before that, I used to look like Meathead from *All in the Family*."

After he ditched the Meathead look, Morrison took the new permed look to the streets of San Diego. He looked good. He also took it back to his hometown of Sydney, Nova Scotia, in the off-season. No offence to the people of my home province, but we're not exactly known as cutting edge when it comes to style. But just like he had to do on the ice from time to time, when it came to style off the ice, Morrison had to set the tone. The curls on this card were just a small part of his look.

"I had a big pink Cadillac with the hair and the Fu Manchu. So I looked like a real uh, a . . . pimp."

In this card, Morrison is clearly wearing a San Diego Mariners sweater. Take note, the sweater has sleeves. Morrison did not sport the sweater, or the sleeves, behind the wheel of his big pink Caddy. "I had the sleeveless suits, the whole thing, that was the fad then."

Which, of course, raises the question: what is a sleeveless suit? "Just like a vest; it's a suit with no arms in it. We had the safari look, that's what was big in the '70s."

And in the '70s Morrison was pretty big on the ice as well. He put up some great numbers in the WHA. The big blueliner racked up a career-high 81 points for San Diego in 1974–75. It was the second of his three straight 20-plus goal seasons.

"I had a few pretty good years in WHA. Scored the 20 goals three years in a row; that was a pretty big feat for a defenceman."

Aside from the sleeveless suit, another thing this card fails to capture is just how tough a player Kevin Morrison was. He put up huge offensive numbers in the WHA. But during his time in the league, Morrison did not spend a huge amount of time in the penalty box. His 143 penalty minutes in San Diego in 1974–75 were the most he ever had in the WHA.

That's because Morrison was a little more of a rebel in his pre–Rebel League days. In 1970–71 with the Eastern League's New Haven Blades, Morrison spent just shy of six complete hours in the penalty box: 348 minutes. How did those PIMs evaporate once Morrison made it to the World League? He says it's pretty simple.

"I kind of fought a lot of the tougher guys that came out of that league that advanced, like [Dave] Schultz and a few of the other guys. So when we got to the higher leagues I'd kind of proved myself against those guys, so they pretty much left me alone.

"I'd probably had maybe eight or 10 fights a year, if that. I didn't really have to go out and establish myself every year so that made a big difference. Being in the earlier leagues, I'd already fought most of them so it didn't have to be done again."

But on occasion it had to be done again. The late Steve Durbano was a legendary tough guy in the 1970s. NHL or WHA, it didn't matter where or when, Durbano was usually ready to go.

If you've ever cruised through old WHA footage on YouTube, you've likely seen this clip. Steve Durbano is going wild, he wants a piece of his opponent, who is sitting in the penalty box. The opponent was Kevin Morrison. Eventually Durbano got within striking distance, and Morrison let him have it. Kevin Morrison delivered one of the cleanest rights of all time.

"That whole skirmish happened and the linesman came over and the referee came over and said, 'Don't do anything. I'm only going to give you two minutes, and you can come right back out on the ice.' But [Durbano] kept coming at me, coming at me and kept hollering at me. And then all of a sudden he kind of glanced me with one punch and I said, 'Enough of this. I don't care if I get kicked out of the game or not. I can't put up with this anymore.' So I hooked him. I got him right on the chin."

The shot counted, it was clean, it was flush. Kevin Morrison could beat you on the ice, he could beat you in the alley. And yes, he could beat you while you were standing on the ice and he was standing in the penalty box. It had its advantages. "You can get a little better foothold," says Morrison.

Morrison looks smooth on the card. He was smooth on the ice, he was smooth off the ice. He had his own look. So did just about everybody else. Morrison says he wasn't the most outlandish guy in a cast of characters. And he is correct. The WHA had all kinds of guys. A lot of them had their own sense of style, that's what comes back to Morrison when he sees this card.

"Billy Goldthorpe—we used to call him Ogie Ogilthorpe, from the movie *Slap Shot*—his afro was almost the width of his shoulders; mine was a baby compared to his."

Morrison also recalls just how good the hockey was in the WHA and what the league meant to hockey then, and perhaps more importantly, what it means to hockey now. "These guys today that are making the millions and millions of dollars can thank the WHA. That's something that they don't do. They don't even recognize us and that's the sad part."

"It'd be nice to be 22 again." If Kevin Morrison were 22 years old today, he'd likely be in for a great payday. No doubt he'd drop a few bucks on a nice ride or two. And while you may be sitting around wondering what happened to that box of old cards at your mother's place, Morrison wonders about some '70s items he used to collect. You traded cards, he traded wheels. The pink Caddy, it's long gone.

"I traded that in for a Lincoln. Every other year I'd trade. I had the Lincoln and then I had an Eldorado. I always loved the big pimp cars."

Hopefully he kept the sleeveless suit.

JOE DALEY 1976–77 OPC #20 (WHA)

The first question that comes to mind when I look at Joe Daley shuffling across his crease is: "Who or what is he trying to stop?" The lights are out, the crease is lit and Daley is ready to go.

This photo alone—the pose, the gear, the logo, the perm—takes you right back to the height of the WHA's rebel years. On one glorious day, or night, we're not quite sure, Joe Daley struck a pose.

"I have no idea when it was taken or how it was taken," says Daley, who played with the Jets for their entire seven-year WHA run.

Back in the day, posing for a card was nothing out of the ordinary. And why would it be, when you were as styling as the then 33-year-old Joe Daley? You should take the time to do it right.

"The earlier ones, when I was in the national league, I know you used to pose for them. They'd come around, you'd sit on a stool or something and that ended up being the one on the card. I think later on, I don't know whether they got one of the local guys to take some pictures or get some action shots from games or what, but some of them were pretty odd ball–ish."

Odd ball–ish, indeed. That's a great way to describe this card. And it's a card that Daley gets to see on a more than regular basis. He's no stranger to his cardboard. In fact for over two decades, he's operated Joe Daley's Sportscards in Winnipeg.

Daley, who also played in the NHL for Pittsburgh, Buffalo and Detroit, sees the '76–77 O-Pee-Chee all the time. And he also sees the reactions on the faces of some younger fans that come by his store, when a father tells his son that the straight-haired guy standing behind the counter once tended goal, '70s perm and all.

"There are a few things hanging around in the store with my picture on it. Of course a dad will point that out to a young child. Then I can see the kid kind of looking out the side of his eye at me, thinking, 'I don't know whether Dad's telling me the truth.'"

Joe is more than ready to admit that his hair on the card was "modified." He had the curly locks and he had the sideburns. This card proves that once upon a time Joe Daley was all '70s rebel. Just like the WHA. "There were various styles and long hair wasn't out of the norm and there are still some guys with an awful lot of hair. Now things are a little different. Guys are making a lot of money so they probably got beauticians that are looking after them from time to time. Back then we just kind of went with the flow and some guys wanted to be a little bit different, and I guess I was just one of those guys."

And he was. And that's what this piece of cardboard tells us over 35 years later. It captures a time when maybe there weren't as many clichés, when players were a little more open to express their style, their swagger. At least in the WHA. "It was different, unique, rebellious, but growing and responding to the wishes of the fans, and that was giving us a chance to provide some pretty good hockey."

And it gave Joe Daley one pretty cool hockey card. However in his younger days it was no big deal. It's not like he was at training camp, tearing through the latest box of O-Pee-Chee trying to pull one of his crease-posing cards out of a pack. "I never really thought much of it," says the three-time AVCO Cup champion. "You don't know at the time that you're getting your picture taken that someday these are going to be the things that people will want to have in their collections."

But now, all these years later, the 1976–77 O-Pee-Chee and his other cards provide a link to some glorious days. "I've accumulated them and it's just neat to be able to look at the cards. It brings back a lot of memories from the time period of the card.

"My cards are not overly priced [Daley's '76–77 will cost you a buck or two] but they're cherished by many people including myself and my family. When people travel across the country, I always tell them to try and go into the shops and pick up a few if they're going to come back through Winnipeg, because I'd certainly buy them off of them; it's always a pleasure for me to autograph one and give it to a smiling kid here in the store."

A smiling kid who's probably asking, 'Did that guy really have all that curly hair?' Don't worry; all those perms didn't cost much anyway. "The good thing about it was my cousin is a hairdresser, so I used to get them at bargain prices."

Norm Beaudin 1974–75 OPC #11 (WHA)

Norm Beaudin is a really nice guy. In conversation, he comes off as a very polite, happy and content man. It's kind of hard to believe that there was a little bit of an undercover-like operation to his past. That a meeting in a dark alley once took place that led to 32-year-old Norm Beaudin ending up on a Winnipeg Jets hockey card in the winter of 1974–75.

In a card standard for the era, Beaudin is striking the classic hockey card pose. "I guess they kept it pretty simple at that time when they took our picture. Just a plain background and that was it. But you know it's ironic, even when I was with the North Stars—I have one when I was with the North Stars—and I can't even remember having it taken. When I was with the Blues, I didn't get one for some reason."

But when he was with the Jets, Beaudin got two cards: one in 1972–73 and then a couple of years later, this beauty from '74–75. And it's the story of what led him to the Jets that we stumble upon when we start talking about this old piece of cardboard.

The story is right there on the back of the card: "He was the first player signed by the Jets." But that sentence on the back of this card only scratches the surface of how Beaudin and the Jets came together. The story begins in Cleveland in the late winter, early spring of 1972.

"Bill Robinson [who signed many of the original Jets] called me. He says, 'We'd like to talk to you.' I says, 'Well, okay.' He said, 'We got something planned here.' He never told me it was Winnipeg or the new league or anything. He just said we'd like to talk to you."

Beaudin figured it never hurts to listen. He met his would-be suitors at a restaurant. Soon though, things ended up in a dark alley. That's when the talk of a new league and a superstar joining it heated up. "We started talking and somehow Bobby Hull's name came up and that triggered something." When Beaudin heard the name Bobby Hull, it lent some legitimacy to the talk of a new league. The fact that Beaudin was in his early 30s and playing in the AHL also made him listen. He was not raking in millions. An athlete's earning potential is limited; he only has so many years to make some cash. So if you hear about a chance to make a little more money while playing with a guy like Bobby Hull, needless to say, your ears perk up.

"When we started talking about Bobby Hull, like I said, it triggered something and I said, 'What are the chances of him jumping?' and he said, 'It's pretty good.'" Then the extra incentive was brought up. "And they made a pretty good offer. So at that time I said, 'Well, if I'm going to stay in Cleveland with the Barons in the American League, why not, you know?'"

The next challenge for Beaudin was to remain quiet. He still had some hockey to play in Cleveland, while thoughts of a bigger payday and playing with Bobby Hull danced around in his head.

"I never divulged anything—at that time, I was with the North Stars organization [the Barons were an affiliate of the Stars] and John Muckler was a coach and manager so I didn't want to talk about it in the dressing room at all because they might have said, 'Well, you're gone.'"

Soon the Barons' season came to an end. Then Beaudin got another call from the Jets. Come to Winnipeg, they said. It wasn't long before Beaudin was on a plane, bound for the Manitoba capital. And then, before he knew it, he wasn't a Baron anymore. He was a Jet.

"We made a deal right then. I think it was April 26 when I signed my contract."

Beaudin's WHA adventure was underway. His tenure began before Bobby Hull's multi-million dollar contract shocked the hockey world. Beaudin took a gamble but he says it was well worth it.

"It was a no-brainer really, because I was maybe tripling my salary and going to the World Hockey Association and then, of course, maybe and hopefully at that time, I said, 'Hopefully Bobby Hull comes.' And he did. It turned out to be great for me. We were on the same line and we were like poetry in motion at the beginning. We had a heck of a line." Beaudin finished in a tie for fourth in the WHA scoring race with 103 points in the league's first season.

This card is the last of Beaudin's hockey career. He ended up skating in the WHA for four seasons before he wrapped up his career with a final season in Switzerland.

These days he lives in Florida, where he is still involved in the game. He runs a hockey shop in an arena and, yes, he sees his old cards all the time from fans and in his own collection. "I've got quite a few. As a matter of fact, I just signed a bunch of them last week. I send them back to the fans."

And the fact that Norm Beaudin appeared on three hockey cards is not lost on him. His hockey life was an adventure. And he has one NHL card and two WHA cards to remind him of the days gone by. "It meant a lot. And it's quite an honour."

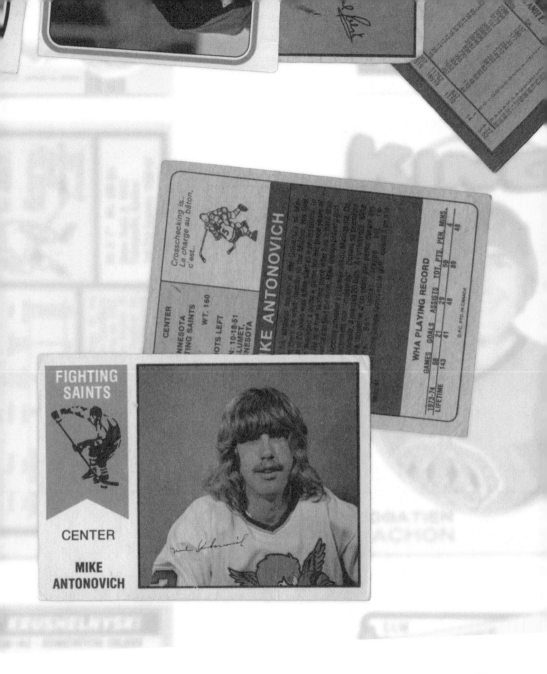

MIKE ANTONOVICH 1974–75 OPC #37 (WHA)

This may be one of the best hockey cards ever made. Forty years after he sat down to strike a quick pose for his first hockey card, Mike Antonovich no longer has that sweet haircut, but he is still laughing about it.

"I've been trying to burn that son of a b for 30 years," he says as he makes his way across the western United States on a scouting trip for the St. Louis Blues. "That was a bad day. What do you call that? A bad hair day?" I'm more inclined to call it an awesome hair day or maybe even the greatest hair day of all time.

"I look at the circumstances more than the hair. The hair was pretty normal then, you know. The circumstances were I didn't know that [picture] was going on that card when they took that picture. I thought it was for our yearbook, you know the Saints. So when the card came out I go what the . . ." says Antonovich before he trails off into another fit of laughter. "A lot of people send me that card to sign. I always want to burn it but I always send it back."

Mike Antonovich clearly gets it. As soon as you talk to him, you like him. He's the kind of guy you'd want to hang out with. He is more than comfortable laughing at his own expense. He knows this card can make for a few giggles and he is more than happy with that. In fact, it made for a few giggles at one St. Louis Blues meeting. "Somebody got a hold of it and blew it up and put it in the office. When I walked into one of our meetings, I said, 'What the hell is that thing doing here?' Right in the meeting, guys are laughing like hell." Who was behind the prank remains a mystery, but Antonovich has a few suspects. He figures it was someone from the amateur scouting department. "It might have been Al MacInnis . . . They had a good laugh over that."

Having a great sense of humour helped Antonovich early in his pro career. He played for the legendary Minnesota Fighting Saints. Some of the names on that team still make hockey fans stand up and pay attention all these years later: Mike "Shakey" Walton, Jack Carlson and Gordie "Machine Gun" Gallant.

"I think you had a combination of a lot of different kinds of characters," says Antonovich, who spent five seasons with the Saints. "We were kind of an off breed. We were just kind of a wild bunch of guys that had a lot of fun playing." Antonovich freely admits that players had a lot more fun back then. But of course they didn't make the big bucks like players do now. During Antonovich's rookie year, he made $20,000, which translates to about $108,000 today. "That was pretty good money. I always thought I was the richest guy in the world."

As the years went on though, the Saints, like a lot of other teams in the WHA, had a tough time paying their bills, and that's when a new dry-land training regiment was introduced to the team. It usually took place every two weeks. It was a sprint to the Saints' financial institution of choice. "It used to be a race to the bank in St. Paul," then there is more laughter. "Everybody went and disappeared because they wanted to be at the bank first because if you weren't in the top 10, sometimes you didn't have any money for two weeks. So we had a couple of those."

But what's better than a cheque in your hand—how about cold hard cash? Once upon a time in Saints land, cash was king. "[The team] had all the money in a paper bag and tried to give us cash and then finally we folded. Guys couldn't take it anymore. We didn't get paid for heck; I don't think we got paid for a month at one stretch. They tried to pay us out of a paper bag at the airport.

"I think Glen Sonmor [the Saints head coach] was holding that bag. He tried to get us to go on one more trip and finally the guys said that's enough. Actually when they folded our team, they wouldn't disperse us to the league because they locked us all out for a long time and then finally after about six weeks they let us go. That was hard . . . I can look back now and just kind of laugh because we were all in the same boat. Even without getting paid, we didn't know if our cheques were cleared, we just played hockey."

These days, Antonovich is in charge of the cheques. Aside from his scouting work with the Blues, he is the mayor of Coleraine, Minnesota, population 2,000. It all started with his buddies saying they needed someone to run for mayor. Antonovich half-heartedly agreed, and voila, the next thing you know, he's a politician. "It's a good volunteer job. You get paid very little but it's been a good experience. It was just kind of on a whim with my buddies asking me to run and do it." You won't see that picture from the '74–75 card on any political signs. That would be fun though, wouldn't it?

The card is a perfect reflection of an era that is now long gone. Back in the '70s, free-wheeling hockey was in and, on this card at least, there was one free-wheeling dude. Look at that hair: it's as untamed as the style of hockey that was played at the time.

"I respect the guys who play today. I respect the game. I always enjoyed the game but you know if you like all that structure and you like someone telling you where to go and what to do, this is a good era for you. For me, I probably would have got turned off and not played. Because the game was pretty simple and all the coverages and everything were simple and basic. It's still basic but they try to make it more than it is."

So then, is this card the perfect reflection of an era and a style of game that is long gone? "I think yeah. If you look even at the National Hockey League teams at that time, there were some loosey-goosey guys in that league too . . . there were some interesting characters. And I think you don't have the characters like they had before. They've taken that out and everybody's kind of vanilla."

There is nothing vanilla about this card, or about Mike Antonovich. He's a mayor, he's a scout and he is one fun fellow to talk to. Before heading even further down the road on another scouting adventure, the man with perhaps the best haircut in hockey history leaves us with one final thought on this gem of a hockey card. "I guess the best thing I can say is, it's brought a lot of laughs to a lot of people. So that's a good thing."

And then Mike Antonovich laughs again.

MIKE PELYK 1974–75 OPC #19 (WHA)

A young Mike Pelyk striking a classic mid-'70s hockey card pose—a pretty innocent, pretty basic card. That's exactly what it was.

"When you look at them now, they're pretty hokey looking," says Pelyk. "But you know that was the state of the nation at that time. Sometimes you stood up straight with your stick and then they tried a few action shots but it was pretty bland stuff, to be honest with you."

"That picture was taken, I was going to say, in the rink that Vancouver played in, the Blazers and Canucks we both played in the same rink, Pacific Coliseum." Which is true: the WHA Blazers and the NHL Canucks shared the same rink while playing in two different leagues. It wasn't tough to tell the teams apart. No one could ever mix up a Blazer with a Canuck. The Blazers were the guys in the awesome orange jerseys. You have to love those uniforms, with the bright "Blazers" running diagonally along the front of the jersey. The unis were fantastic—as long as you weren't one of the guys who had to wear them. "Hey I've seen worse things, right?"

Pelyk ended up in Blazers orange thanks to a lot of green. In the summer of 1974, he was having dinner at the home of Maple Leafs teammate Brian Glennie. All of a sudden the phone rang: Pelyk's agent, Alan Eagleson, wanted to talk.

"He said, 'Look, I got this paperwork. I think it's something you might be interested in. They're offering you a lot of money and blah blah blah.' I said, 'I'm having dinner at Brian Glennie's house and when I leave dinner I'll call you back and we can talk about it.'"

Soon enough Ealgeson filled Pelyk in on the offer. The WHA's Cincinnati Stingers were offering him a deal worth a ton of money. Well, tons of money for a 26-year-old in the summer of 1974. The Stingers offered Pelyk a one-million dollar, seven-year contract. "I was shocked. I was absolutely shocked."

Mike Pelyk had a decision to make: take the WHA cash or play for less with the Toronto Maple Leafs. Pelyk had grown up in Toronto; he wanted to be a Leaf for as long as he could remember; he'd spent his first seven NHL seasons on the Buds' blue line.

"I guess the first thing is, I never wanted to leave Toronto. I tried like crazy to get a better deal than what they were offering with [Leafs GM] Jim Gregory. And Jim said, 'I just can't go any farther,' and I said, 'Look Jim, this is too good a deal to pass up. So you know I gotta do what's right for myself.' But I didn't really want to leave."

Pelyk did leave. He was off to the WHA, but not Cincinnati. The Stingers would not start play in the WHA until the '75–76 season. Like it says on the back of the card, Pelyk was loaned to the Blazers for a year. That's how he ended up wearing orange on this sweet card.

"We didn't have that good a team. We actually missed the playoffs by two points. I was there for the year and I was actually thinking, 'What am I going to do when I go to Cincinnati' because it's a brand new team, right? At that time there was some discussion with Vancouver about actually trying to stay in Vancouver and maybe go to the Canucks. But they just couldn't make the numbers work."

So Pelyk was off to Cinci, but just for a year. After one year with the Stingers, he returned to the Leafs organization. He split the next two seasons between the Leafs and the minors. After the '77–78 season, the Leafs offered Pelyk a two-way deal. He walked away from the game. He made a comeback attempt with the Buffalo Sabres in 1980. It didn't work out, and that was it for Pelyk's hockey career. He eventually found a career in real estate. He's still in it.

When Pelyk thinks of this card, it's not the pose that sticks out or the orange uniform. It's the million-dollar contract he took that led him away from the Leafs and to the WHA. "It was a good experience. The only part I regret is actually leaving to go to the WHA. If I had it all to do over again, I probably would have signed for whatever I could have signed for and tried to prove my worth in Toronto. But sometimes you make decisions, they aren't always the right ones . . . but you've got to live with your decisions, right?"

Pelyk made that decision almost four decades ago. It led to two years in the WHA and one outstanding hockey card. He is still amazed that

people come up to him with his old cards, looking for signatures. His family is pretty amazed with his old cards too. "They say, 'Did you wear a wig then, Dad?' My granddaughter goes, 'Oh Papa, you used to have a lot of hair right? Is that your real hair?'"

For the record, yes it is.

John Garrett 1985–86 OPC #220

They call him Cheech. Thousands of hockey fans from across North America know him as a staple on Vancouver Canucks broadcasts. But once upon a time, John Garrett was destined for the Canucks front office. Or so it seemed.

In 1985, Garrett's age was starting to catch up to him, and the Canucks crease was becoming very crowded.

THE GOALIES — Chapter Four

Richard Brodeur, still hot off the Canucks' run all the way to the 1982 Stanley Cup Final, was the number-one man in Vancouver. Plus a couple of up-and-comers, Wendell Young and Frank Caprice, were pushing for time in the Canucks' net. That's when then Canucks general manager Harry Neale came up to Garrett and made a proposal.

"They kind of wanted to phase me out and I still had a year left on my contract. So Harry came to me, and he didn't have an assistant GM. So he said, 'What would you think? You know we'll give you an extra year and we'll make the money work for you. And I'd like to hire you as my assistant GM,'" says Garrett, who seemed to like the idea. There was, however, just one catch. And it was a big one. Neale laid things on the line for his goaltender.

"The only big thing is I don't know whether I'm going to have a job," Neale told his 'tender. And of course it turned out he didn't. In May 1985, Harry Neale got canned; so much for Garrett's future in the front office. "Had Harry kept his job I would have been an assistant GM," Garrett says.

However the folks at O-Pee-Chee must have figured

they had a scoop, so they went with it. "NOW ASSISTANT GENERAL MANAGER" is on the front of Garrett's final hockey card. It would have been nice, could have been fun, but it never happened.

"That's as far as I got, 'now assistant general manager,' and I got into broadcasting the very next year," says the man who finished up his professional career with the Canucks AHL affiliate, the Fredericton Express, in 1985–86.

And that was it for Garrett's hockey card tenure as well. His '85–86 O-Pee-Chee may incorrectly predict his future career, but it does perfectly capture the style of a typical 1980s goalie. Garrett has it all—the hair, the 'stache, but most of all, the towel. Any self-respecting goalie assigned to back-up duty on any given night during the 1980s had to have the towel. Extra marks to Garrett for colour coordination.

"Oh yeah, no baseball hat. You had the towel around the neck and when the other guy came over you'd throw the towel off and in you'd go."

While sporting the towel on back-up duty, Garrett could sit on the end of the bench, thanks to the smaller equipment of the '80s, and open and close the door, while chirping away at the players on the ice, most of the time.

One classic arena didn't provide a spot on the bench for Garrett when he was on back-up duty. But with diversity often comes opportunity. And in this case a terrific story. Goalie gear of the past may not have been lightweight; Garrett figures it could weigh around 40 pounds by the end of a night. But it did help out in other areas, like food storage.

Back-up goalies have been known to take a bite or two over the years. Jamie McLennan tells of his heavy back-up appetite in his excellent book, *The Best Seat in the House*. John Garrett had a bit of an appetite as well.

"We were playing in Quebec and back in those days in the old Colisée, and I talk about the spare goalie opening the door and closing the door, there you didn't have to," begins Garrett. "It was an old rink. You walked from the dressing room onto the bench and the spare goalie sat in kind of the hallway there in behind. So you weren't really on the bench. The coach really couldn't see you. He was out a little farther and it was pretty convenient."

Convenient for what? Maybe sneaking an extra glimpse up into the stands? For taking a snooze? For uninhibited daydreaming? No. It was convenient for a man who had an appetite in the middle of a professional hockey game. "They had great hot dogs in Quebec City, as everyone knows. So every now and then the trainer would get me a hot dog."

Now try to picture this in today's game. The players, for the most part, are nutrition freaks. Most likely wouldn't eat a hot dog in the middle of July, let alone in the middle of an actual game. Go back a few decades, and it wasn't an issue, at least not for John Garrett. The question is, how do you eat a hot dog without getting caught? Sure, you may be just out of the eye line of the head coach, but someone will see you. Not if you're a hot dog stealth like John Garrett though. He knew just how to take advantage of a giant set of leather goalie pads.

"I'd sit there and I'd have it in my pads. And every now and then, turn away and have a bite of the hot dog."

Simple enough. Take a quick bite; stuff it back down the pads. Repeat until the entire hot dog is consumed. But on one night at the Colisée, Garrett got the call before the entire hot dog found the bottom of his stomach.

"Sure enough, one game Dan Bouchard decided he'd had enough and for no apparent reason—'cause you could tell, you're the back-up goalie: if the score is bad you'd get rid of the hot dog . . . A goal went in and he just came storming off the ice. And I had to go in. I had the hot dog in the pads and couldn't get rid of it," says Garrett. "I strapped up the pads and the hot dog stayed."

In a split second John Garrett, professional goaltender, made up his mind. He was going into the crease, and the hot dog was going with him. "If you weren't playing, your pads were a little looser, so you had [the hot dog] tucked down the pads. So when [Bouchard] came charging over, you know everybody's looking down at me, so I can't just throw the hot dog away. So I just push it down, tighten the pads up and in I go."

John Garrett was thrown into the crease in front of thousands at the historic Colisée. He was stopping pucks, cutting down angles and gliding from post to post. He was doing all of this with a hot dog stuffed down his pads the entire time.

How good was John Garrett at concealing hot dogs? Very good: perhaps the best in the history of the game. The hot dog never saw the ice. It stayed tucked deep down in his pads for the duration of the game. "It's pretty tight in there," Garrett notes nonchalantly.

The hot dog finally made it out well after the final buzzer.

"After the game you wait until everybody leaves. I'm sitting there pretending like I'm really upset that the game didn't go our way and wait until everybody goes and then undo the pads and there's the hot dog. It wasn't edible after that."

The whole thing sounds like a shrewd move. Something an assistant general manager in the making might pull off. When Garrett looks at his old hockey cards, you never know what stories may pop up. He laughs at the haircuts and marvels at just how small his old equipment was compared to the Michelin men we now see.

"I look at those old hockey cards and gosh, my arms are . . . You know I had decent size arms, but holy Christ, they look like toothpicks. And my shoulders and the pants that don't droop around your ass so that nothing that goes though your legs goes in," says Garrett, laughing. "It is a whole new game."

As for the note about his managerial future on his '85–86 O-Pee-Chee, Garrett doesn't get too many people mistaking him for the front office type. He is more than well known as a broadcaster. However someone, somewhere, really did believe that once upon a time, John Garrett was Mr. Front Office. And someone, until recently, still did.

"Wikipedia—I had to correct it. It said I was the assistant general manager for a year with the Vancouver Canucks, so I had to go into Wikipedia and edit my Wikipedia page." Surely that '85–86 O-Pee-Chee was to blame.

MICHEL DION 1984–85 OPC #173

When you're a kid you are drawn to certain types of things. I'm sure I'm not alone when I say that goalie cards always stood out for me. A cool mask was always a sure thing to draw your attention. Michel Dion's mask always did the trick.

Dion's mask was different; at least it was in my 10-year-old eyes. And not only was it different, it flowed perfectly with that black and gold Penguins uniform. The colours of Dion's mask, his Pens uniform and even the border of this '84–85 card all work together flawlessly.

The mask came courtesy of mask designer Michel Lefebvre, who made Dion's masks dating all the way back to his WHA days. "One day in my second year in Quebec during training camp [Michel] shows up at the hotel room and knocks on the door and he's got the mask. And he says, 'I thought maybe you'd like to try this. I took your mold and added an extension to make sure your neck's covered.'" Dion put on the mask and it fit like a glove. When he signed with the Penguins, he took the mask with him.

"I had a friend of mine in Pittsburgh paint the mask the Penguin colours so it would match the uniform, and the rest was history. I just decided to wear the mask. It covered the throat. It was solid, more solid than any other mask I'd worn before as far as protection. And I probably looked good. Some people were starting to say it kind of looks like a Penguins face so I said, 'Well, we didn't have that in mind but if that's the way you guys see it, good for you,'" says Dion, now a golf instructor on Hilton Head Island.

Take your pick, it looked like a penguin or it looked like a duck. Most would argue duck. That's why the mask, sported by Dion and a number of 'tenders at the time, including Mike Liut, was called the duck bill mask.

There's a reason Dion and his duck bill look like they're in trouble on the front of this card. It's because they were. To say Dion was slightly overworked in the Penguins crease during the '83–84 season would be something of an understatement. Look at the stats on the back of the card for '83–84. Dion has a 5.33 goals against average in 30 games. That's nothing to write home about. What the stats don't show is that the '83–84 Pens gave up 390 goals, the highest total in the NHL.

"I guess Kenny Dryden wrote a book about goaltenders one time and he separated goalies into two categories: good bad-team goalies and the good good-team goalies. And I would qualify me as a good bad-team goalie." And when you're a good bad-team goalie, you're not just stopping the initial shot and then pleasantly watching your defense clear the rebound away. You're stopping the rebound, then the rebound from that rebound, and the rebound from that rebound. And then there are the uneven breaks.

"Your goals against average isn't really going to impress anybody, but the quality of save-making is probably superior. But you're not going to get credit for it because you just get so much work that you're by yourself a lot of times and there's just a lot of goals you're just not going to have any chances on. And if they're not going to have to beat you, they'll just beat your team, slide the puck in an open net and it goes against your average. But a guy that knows goaltending would look at things like that more than things like save percentage or other stats."

During his final year in Pittsburgh, Dion saw the future. Hope had finally arrived for the long struggling Penguins in the form of a young Mario Lemieux. He was fresh out of the Quebec League. As one of the few French players on the Pens, it was Dion's job to take the young Lemieux under his wing. "I was there to hang around with him the first few months. He didn't speak a lot of English and I was kind of the only guy on the team that spoke French so I took him around and introduced him to people and made sure he was safe. He was only 17 years old."

Lemieux may have only been a teenager, but his talent was world class. We all know that Mario move on the breakaway—fake the forehand and a quick deke to the backhand—and Dion got to see it up close in one of Mario's first practices with the Penguins.

"I remember the first time he had a breakaway on me. He tried the deke move that he used to score on every time and I'd never seen a move like that. I ended up stopping him but I remember thinking to myself, 'Man, was that a good move. I've never seen that before, not from Gretzky, not from anybody.' Of course every time he tried it in games he scored. The other goalies had never seen that either. And I remember telling Eddie Johnston, 'The kid's good. He's got moves I've never seen. I stopped him today but I won't stop him every time, that's for sure.' He was truly talented. Obviously Gretzky and him were in a league of their own."

Mario's first season in Pittsburgh was Dion's last. He retired after the '84–85 campaign. He ended up playing professional hockey for 11 years. However it wasn't his only sporting option. Dion could have carved out a career for himself in baseball.

Look at his '84–85 card again: he's trying to stop a puck. It's kind of the same position a desperate catcher might use to stop a wild pitch in baseball. Once upon a time, Michel Dion was a prospect in the Montreal Expos organization as a catcher. There was only one problem. About a year after Dion joined the Expos organization, another young prospect showed up on the scene. His name was Gary Carter. As in future Hall of Famer Gary Carter.

"I walked into batting practice one day and he hit 10 straight balls over the left field fence and the harder the pitcher threw, the harder he hit the ball. And I said to myself this is out of my league offensively. Defensively he had things to learn and as a matter of fact they used me to help him out because my hands were much quicker. He was a diamond in the rough, so to speak, defensively. He wasn't polished when he first came in but he was obviously a tremendous talent. And of course with the bat, his talent was obvious. The guy was going to be a great hitter and a home run hitter."

Dion had a decision to make: would he try to beat out Carter for a job, or would he strap on the pads again and give hockey another go? When he joined the Expos organization, he skipped out on an entire year of hockey. No matter, he chose to try his luck stopping pucks instead of catching fastballs.

It was a fantastic decision. That young catching prospect that Dion thought had a knack for hitting the long ball went on to hit 324 Major League home runs. Years later, Carter and Dion would cross paths again at the Montreal Forum. The catcher was in the crowd; the 'tender was in the crease for the visiting Quebec Nordiques.

"Gary was on the boards at the end of the game. And I hear this guy calling me and his thumb was in a cast because he had gotten his hand operated on. He had problems with his thumb and there were a bunch of people around him. I recognized him and went and shook hands with him and we talked a little bit. It was good to see him, and I told him, I said, 'I told you we'd both make it.'"

They did. In fact they were both All-Stars. Carter was an 11 time All-Star and Dion played in the NHL All-Star Game in 1982.

Who knows, if Dion had chosen baseball maybe he and Gary Carter could have had cards in the same baseball card set. But he went with hockey, and that's what led to him donning his classic mask on his final hockey card, his '84–85 O-Pee-Chee.

"When I was a kid, I was impressed by good looks and goalies who looked good. And I wanted to look good too. So it's kind of a look thing," chuckles Dion. "In some ways your mask is more well known than you are, but that's okay. If it makes somebody happy and they can collect cards and like that card because of it, then it's one more way that your career can serve and help people out even after you are done with it."

1982-83
HIGHLIGHT
FAITS SAILLANTS

CORRADO MICALEF
Red Wings • Goalie/Gardien

116

MICALEF BLANKS ISLANDERS
DETROIT, Dec. 8 — Goaltender Corrado Micalef posted the first shutout of his National Hockey League career tonight, blanking the Stanley Cup Islanders, 2-0. Micalef faced 26 shots in the triumph, including a penalty shot stop on Clark Gillies. The victory was the fifth of the season for the Red Wings.

MICALEF BLANCHIT LES ISLANDERS
DÉTROIT, le 8 décembre — Le gardien Corrado Micalef réussit ce soir son premier blanchissage dans la Ligue nationale. Il blanchit les champions de la Coupe Stanley, les Islanders, par une marque de 2 à 0. Micalef arrêta 26 lancers durant ce match, y compris un lancer de punition de Clark Gillies. Ce fut la cinquième victoire de la saison pour les Red Wings.

©1983 O-Pee-Chee Ptd. in Canada-Imprimé au Canada

© 1983 NHLPA

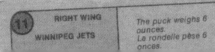

CORRADO MICALEF 1983–84 OPC #116

It's the mask. It has always been the mask. As a kid I was always drawn to this card simply because of Corrado Micalef's mask. Or was it a mask? I had never seen anything like it, and come to think of it, I haven't seen a lot of masks like that one since 1983. It was almost like a helmet/mask combo. Look at the top of that thing: it looks like someone took an old hockey helmet and glued it on top of a mask.

"It's different," Micalef says bluntly. "It's really molded to your face and it's got a bit of a creepy look to it. And when I look at it, I'm just amazed at how much of my neck is exposed, you see the flesh. I wasn't the only one wearing that kind of mask; a few goalies had it in the league, something similar. In that era the masks were starting to change too. But it's got a unique look—it just comes around your chin and all the way back to the top of the head and rounding features. It's got a little bit of a horror look to it."

It is kind of scary. The credit for the design, Micalef says, goes to Ernie Higgins of Boston, who designed it during Micalef's final year of Junior. It turns out that the scariest thing about the mask during the 1980–81 Quebec Major Junior Hockey League season was the guy wearing it. Micalef went 35–26–3 for the Sherbrooke Castors in the regular season and earned a spot on the QMJHL's first All-Star Team. Then things got even better. He was loaned to the Quebec League champs, the Cornwall Royals, for the Memorial Cup. Micalef went 3–0 at the tournament and led the Royals to the 1980–81 Memorial Cup title. Then Micalef and his mask hit the pro ranks.

Micalef doubled up, hockey card style, during the 1983–84 season. His regular rookie card was inserted into packs everywhere and so was this highlight card. The mask takes centre stage, but the reason for the card is pretty cool as well. Corrado Micalef, playing for the lowly 1982–83 Detroit Red Wings, shutout the Stanley Cup champion New York Islanders. And for an eternity, he has the cardboard evidence to prove it.

"That game, you don't forget that. They were the champs and that was their era. Right from '80–84 I believe, a lot of great players on that team." There were a ton of great players on those New York Islanders. Bossy, Nystrom, Trottier, Potvin, just to name a few.

"I was nervous about playing them that night and I remember [Detroit defenseman] Jim Schoenfeld telling me in the shower in the morning, 'Just go out there and shut the door on them.' You know just like a remark that way, and I actually went out and got a shutout. And there was actually a penalty shot in that game and I stopped that, so it was a great, great memory."

On the back of the card, the penalty shot is duly noted: "Micalef faced 26 shots in the triumph, including a penalty shot stop on Clark Gilles." If you were going to shutout the defending Stanley Cup champs, why wouldn't you want to stop a future Hall of Famer like Clark Gillies in a one-on-one duel?

"He kind of faked the shot and came up and tried to pump fake me and go to his backhand and I came across with him and stayed with him and got my pad on it . . . You don't forget that kind of moment."

The card is a reminder of that moment. And a reminder of Micalef's NHL career, which turned out to be rather short. After the 1985–86 season, Micalef's days in an NHL crease, much like his shutout against the Islanders, were history. The Wings had a crowded net, with goalies like Greg Stefan, Mark Laforest and Glen Hanlon in the mix. After splitting time between the NHL and the AHL in '85–86, Micalef had a decision to make. He had an offer to go to Switzerland and a mere 24 hours to make up his mind. He decided to go to Europe.

"I thought I'd give it a try and actually ended up staying there for most of 20 years." A quick decision led to a very long European career for Micalef. He ended up playing overseas until 2001–02.

"I got to live in four different countries and play in different leagues and it's amazing the amount of players that end up over there. Some guys I played with are guys that you're following and they come and finish up their careers there or guys that have given up on the NHL, that weren't getting a break." Micalef played in France, Italy and Germany, among other stops.

Once his playing career came to an end, he ended up back in Canada. He caught on as an assistant coach with the QMJHL's PEI Rockets while studying at the University of Prince Edward Island.

Thirty years after his NHL career began, Micalef still looks back on his time in the game as an amazing period in his life. He had a few years in Detroit, then almost two decades in Europe. Who could have predicted that? He spent most of his career in Europe, but he is always reminded of his time in the NHL thanks to his hockey cards, especially his '83–84 highlight card.

"That card pops up quite a bit so it's always fun to see that. I think I have three hockey cards out there and I still receive cards for autographs. Amazingly 30 years later, I'm still receiving cards."

And he's still getting comments on the mask as well.

Murray Bannerman

Ht: 5'11" Wt: 184 Shoots: L 1st Pro Season: 1977-78
Acquired: Trade with Canucks
Born: 4-27-57, St. Francis, Ontario
Home: Thunder Bay, Ontario

32

NHL record / Fiche dans la LNH

YEAR	TEAM	GP	MIN	GA	SO	AVG
77-78	Canucks	1	20	0	0	0.00
80-81	Black Hawks	15	865	62	0	4.30
81-82	Black Hawks	29	1671	116	1	4.17
82-83	Black Hawks	41	2460	127	4	3.10
83-84	Black Hawks	56	3335	188	2	3.38
NHL Totals		142	8,351	493	7	3.54

Stopped 34 shots in helping Hawks to a season opening
4-3 win over Blues, 10-5-83. Murray was the starting
goaltender for the Campbell Conf. in the 1984 All Star
Game.
Durant le match inaugural du 5-10-83, il bloqua 34 lancers pour aider les Hawks à vaincre les Blues 4 à 3.
Murray fut le gardien partant de la conférence Campbell
lors du match des étoiles de 1984.

Murray Bannerman
BLACK HAWKS
G

Murray Bannerman 1984–85 OPC #32

The colours jump right off the card. There's the classic Blackhawks jersey. And that mask is one of the best of the 1980s. But what stands out to Murray Bannerman when he looks at his 1984–85 O-Pee-Chee? A lack of fundamentals.

"It's funny because I spent a lot of time coaching youth hockey after I retired here. And I was always telling goalies when they move side to side, move around the net, that they always want to keep their stick on the ice, so they could be ready for anything that could happen. And I look at that hockey card and my stick is about a foot off the ice," says the former All-Star. "I guess that's the first thing, surprisingly enough, that's the first thing that comes to mind when I look at that hockey card."

In my mind, Bannerman was big-time back when I was a kid. That's likely because he popped up on my parents' TV every spring in the playoffs. At least in my mind, he popped up on the TV every year in the playoffs. It seemed to me the Blackhawks always faced off against the Oilers in the chase for the Stanley Cup. In reality though, the Blackhawks and Oilers only faced off two times in the playoffs during Bannerman's time in Chicago, in the spring of 1983 and the spring of 1985. The Oilers won both times.

"It wasn't fun, especially going into Edmonton and playing those guys." And why would it be? The '80s Oilers were an absolute powerhouse. "I think if you look back through the '80s, if you look at that '82 to '86 type of time frame, I think with the team we had in Chicago, we were probably the second-best team in the league."

But if you wanted out of the Campbell Conference in the 1980s, you had to go through the Oilers. You had to stop Gretzky, Messier, Kurri, Anderson and Coffey. That's a tough task for any 'tender. Bannerman tried his best to take it all in stride.

"It really wasn't any different than any other game. Yeah they were better, and you knew you were going to face a lot of quality scoring chances, but I mean your preparation as a goaltender is pretty much the same every game. You focus on the things that you as an individual need to do to be successful and try to block out all the other stuff that goes with it."

As a kid another thing that drew me to Bannerman was his mask. Bannerman had a mask that made him stand out. And it looked dang cool on a piece of cardboard. "The guy that made the mask was Greg Harrison," says Bannerman. "Basically what happened is I told him what I wanted, which was the Blackhawk emblem. 'However you think you could fit that on the mask, that's what I'd like to do.' He pretty much came up with the design. It's kind of neat. It was a little unusual for the time. There were guys that had maybe a design on their mask but it wasn't related to that particular team . . . I wore that mask throughout my whole career. And guys were going to the cages. I think that kind of adds to the remembrance of it, because when everybody else was going to the cage I stuck with that."

Yes, by the time Bannerman got towards the end of his NHL career in '86–87, his mask was a relic of the past. The cage-fibreglass combo that was soon to become mainstream was starting to pop up. It had the promise of better sightlines and better protection. Take a close look at Bannerman's mask. It is molded right to his face. Imagine taking a puck off that thing, it would sting.

"It hurt like hell. I got hit in the head many times . . . One time, surprisingly enough, it was against Edmonton in the playoffs. [Glenn] Anderson hit me in the head and I was out cold: kind of above the eyes, about the middle of the forehead. And back in those days they'd give you a little smelling salts and get you back in the game and you'd finish up the game. You know, the next day when you got a headache they said, 'Take a couple Tylenol and get back out there.' A little bit [of a] different time in that respect."

It was in the mid-'80s that Bannerman made his mark in Chicago. He'll tell you, "I had a decent career. I wouldn't say it was great by any stretch of the imagination. But it was a decent career." In Chicago, one moment from that decent career still lives on to this day. It happened in

April 1985. Murray Bannerman stoned the Minnesota North Stars' Keith Acton on a breakaway in the 1985 playoffs.

Play-by-play announcer Pat Foley made the call: "Acton moving right in all alone, the shot, *BANNERMAN* did it again!" It was a stellar pad save. The Blackhawks went on to win the best-of-seven series in six games.

"If you talk to people that were hockey fans in the '80s in Chicago, they'll remember that and they'll associate me with that. So it gives you maybe a little bit more notoriety or fame, if you want to call it that, than you might have had if that wouldn't have been the case."

Bannerman, it's a name, but it's also a signature call, as in *BANNERMAN!* "Being in sales, I see people who were fans back in that era and that's the one thing they remember. I don't think they remember a lot about the games or necessarily how we did or where we were but they do remember that."

BANNERMAN! pops up everywhere: on the street, in a sales meeting and on the golf course at a Blackhawks alumni event. The ex-goalie was recently re-hashing old times with former Blackhawk Bill Gardner. Murray lives in Chicago now, but at the time of the golf event, he hadn't been around Chicago in about four years.

"Pat [Foley] comes up and says, 'Hey, there's the two guys that made me famous.'" Bannerman knew what was coming from Foley. Gardner knew what was coming from Foley. The other guys sitting at the table had no idea what Foley was talking about. They knew about *BANNERMAN!* But two guys who made Foley famous? "The other guys at the table are kind of looking around, 'What do you mean two guys?' Because unbeknownst to a lot of people, that breakaway that Acton had, Billy was the guy that gave the puck away and gave up the breakaway."

Bannerman bailed out Gardner, Foley made the call and the *BANNERMAN* name lives on. If you have a moment, try to find a clip of that Gardner giveaway. It would make any coach cringe: a no-look pass at the other team's blue line. Ouch.

That save is a great memory for Bannerman. The cards are nice, but the old goalie doesn't obsesses over them. "I don't have any that I specifically kept for myself."

Like a lot of old goalies, he doesn't strap on the pads much now. In fact, he hasn't worn them in about five years. But once you get him talking about this old O-Pee-Chee, he's right back out there.

BANNERMAN!

ED STANIOWSKI 1976–77 OPC #104

He's young. He has that sly grin. He has the great hair. He has the old glove. The old blocker. The old pads. He's a rookie, about to take on the hockey world, but hockey is just one small part of Ed Staniowski's life.

"To get yourself placed on a hockey card was pretty exciting. Especially the first time you see it. For me I wasn't too pleased about the photograph on it . . . a lot of flowing hair," says Staniowski, known these days as Lieutenant Colonel Staniowski, a veteran member of the Canadian Forces.

"I remember when the photograph was taken. It was part of a series of photographs that were done in St. Louis during training camp that year." Soon enough, the young St. Louis 'tender learned he was in hockey card heaven, or at least, hockey card photographer heaven. "The thing about St. Louis that a lot of people don't know is, almost all of the rookie cards—not almost all of them but a large, large number of them—the photographs that were taken before they started doing action shots, were done in the old St. Louis Arena. If you look at the backdrop, you look at most of the teams other than St. Louis are in visitor sweaters. And if you look at the background when there are action shots, a lot of times you'll see Blues players in their home sweaters in the photograph."

A fair share of Blues home white sweaters do pop up on the '76–77 set, but why St. Louis? "I was told that a lot of the photographs initially were taken in St. Louis because the lighting was so good. I remember they had a real powerful strobe there that the photographers could plug into right down by the boards, and when they hit their camera, POOF. I remember as a goaltender you notice those things, big flashes."

Soon enough Staniowski's hockey card began to find its way into the hands of anxious kids throughout North America. One of those kids approached Ed Staniowski on a cold winter's night as he was making his way out of the old St. Louis Arena.

"At the time I was dating a St. Louis girl and as we were heading up the ramp and heading to the car after a game, a young boy of about 9 or 10 is standing there with his parents. And he says, 'Mr. Staniowski, can I have your autograph?'" The fact that a kid called him mister is still a bit amazing to the Lieutenant Colonel all these years later.

"I just turned 20 and I'm walking out to my new sports car in my best suit and here's this young man calling me Mr. Staniowski, and I'm barely out of my teens myself. He says, 'Can I have your autograph?' I said, 'Certainly young man I'd be happy to sign your card for you.' And he looks up at me and he stares at me and he stares at me and he says, 'You know I have about eight or nine of your cards.' And I said, 'Oh, really' and with a little bit of self pride I said, 'I must be one of your favourites, eh?'"

This is when harsh reality enters the picture. Kids often speak the truth. This one did. "He looked up at me and he said, 'No, actually. I can't trade them for shit.' I looked at his parents and I said, 'It's probably way past his bedtime. You better get him home.' Anyway the long and short of it was we had a good laugh about it, but it put things into perspective very early in my career about the game, what's important. [The game is] important to a lot of people but the sports page is a long way from the front page of the newspaper."

The front page of the newspaper is where Staniowski's current line of work usually ends up. His playing days came to an end in 1984–85. Then it was on to an entirely different career. As a kid he had always wanted to head into the military. "I had hoped when I was attending high school out in Saskatchewan that I would be accepted and attend Royal Military College. As it turns out, I got drafted by the Blues. I say, tongue in cheek, that I'm one of the few people that can say I couldn't join the army because I got drafted."

Eventually he did join, and he's been a member of the Canadian Forces for over 25 years, serving with pride around the globe alongside an entirely new set of teammates. "There's that same commonality, that same brotherhood or sisterhood, if you will, from serving members of the forces. And I've been very fortunate to have 26, 27 years now of a second career that has allowed me to have that same closeness with the people that I work with."

So to some, Ed Staniowski is the hockey player. To others, Ed Staniowski is Lieutenant Colonel. Sometimes, however, he is both. "A couple of times I went over to Afghanistan wearing a dual hat, both as a service member but also escorting the Stanley Cup with the NHL guys that went over. It was a real privilege for me to see my two worlds come together, the military and hockey."

Staniowski went over with a large group of former NHLers including the likes of Tiger Williams, the late Bob Probert and Mark Napier. It was all to have a little fun and to say thanks for all that the Canadian Forces do.

"Those two brotherhoods and sisterhoods coming together, it's pretty impressive. Pretty humbling to see that commonality that was there, and that genuine respect for each other."

And even in Afghanistan, halfway around the globe, a little cardboard entered the equation. "Who goes off to war in Afghanistan and takes their hockey cards with them? But I'll tell you: people were producing hockey cards over there and getting the NHL guys to sign them. You couldn't be further away from a sheet of ice . . . you've got young men and women pulling out hockey cards, wearing their hockey sweaters of their favourite team and getting them autographed. It was amazing to see."

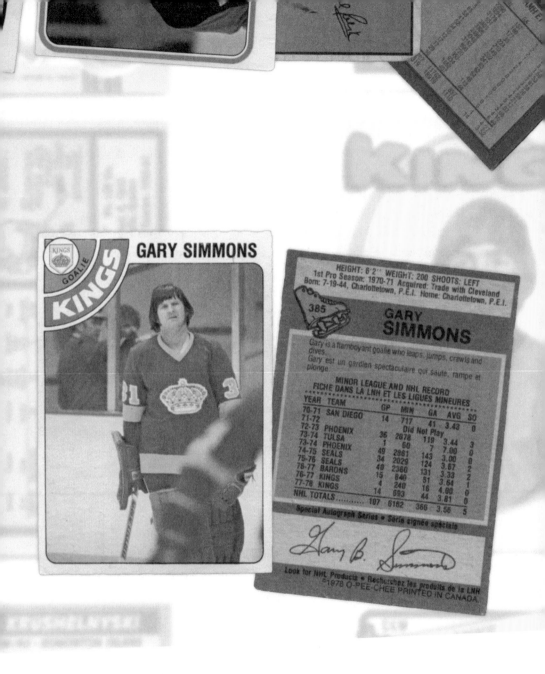

GARY SIMMONS

HEIGHT: 6'2" WEIGHT: 200 SHOOTS: LEFT
1st Pro Season: 1970-71 Acquired: Trade with Cleveland
Born: 7-19-44, Charlottetown, P.E.I. Home: Charlottetown, P.E.I.

385

GARY SIMMONS

Gary is a flamboyant goalie who leaps, jumps, crawls and dives.
Gary est un gardien spectaculaire qui saute, rampe et plonge.

MINOR LEAGUE AND NHL RECORD
FICHE DANS LA LNH ET LES LIGUES MINEURES

YEAR	TEAM	GP	MIN	GA	AVG	SO
70-71	SAN DIEGO	14	717	41	3.43	0
71-72			Did Not Play			
72-73	PHOENIX					
73-74	TULSA	36	2078	119	3.44	3
73-74	PHOENIX	1	60	7	7.00	0
74-75	SEALS	49	2961	143	3.00	0
75-76	SEALS	34	2029	124	3.67	2
76-77	BARONS	40	2360	131	3.33	2
76-77	KINGS	4	840	51	3.64	1
77-78	KINGS	14	693	44	4.00	0
NHL TOTALS		107	6162	366	3.56	5

Special Autograph Series • Série signée spéciale

Look for NHL Products • Recherchez les produits de la LNH
©1978 O-PEE-CHEE PRINTED IN CANADA

GARY SIMMONS 1978–79 OPC #385

Gary Simmons has a strange look on his face on his '78–79 O-Pee-Chee card, like he's pondering some sort of question. Perhaps he is thinking about his future. The one question I ask myself when I look at Simmons's final hockey card is: where's the mask?

During his playing days, Gary Simmons's cobra mask, one of the all-time great goalie masks, never made an appearance on a single one of his hockey cards. And that is a shame. The mask is one of the greatest ever worn in the National Hockey League. It featured a giant cobra painted on the front, stretching across the entire face of the mask. Hockey card collectors never got to see the mask until recently when a number of new sets have Simmons sporting the snake mask.

Simmons can't tell you why his mask never made it on to his cards. He can't tell you what he was thinking about on the front of his '78–79 card either, but he can tell you that his old cobra mask was a big deal then, and it's a big deal now too.

"I know the masks now are really, really jumping. There's a lot of interest in the masks. There's a lot of people making replicas and a lot of people looking to buy them. You know I think our masks back then, nothing against the ones today, but ours back then, they were awesome."

Take a look at the back of Simmons's card; the guy played in some rather exotic locations. What the card doesn't tell you is that he played in some non-exotic climates as well. Like in Newfoundland, where he won a Herder Cup. As for the exotic locations, his first real professional hockey home, after a quick stop in San Diego, was in Phoenix. And that's where he got the name that led to one of the greatest masks the game has ever seen.

"The first game I ever played there, a writer came in after the game and I remember we had beat Salt Lake 6–2, and he said, 'Man, you were like a snake out there riding around on the ice.' And there was a guy named Bob Barlow, Blah Blah Barlow, sitting like two [stalls] down from me and he said, 'Yeah, just like a cobra.' It was in the newspaper the next day and I've had that name since 1972."

The style also stuck. The bio on the back of the card kind of describes a cobra as well. "Gary is a flamboyant goalie who leaps, jumps, crawls and dives."

When the Cobra nickname caught on in Phoenix, he started selling cobra t-shirts. He brought his t-shirt idea with him when he finally made it to the NHL, with the California Seals in 1974–75, at a not-so-young 30 years old. No doubt, that had a little something to do with his style and personality. "I never forgot where I came from," he says. "And maybe part of that is because it took me so long to get to the NHL. I didn't play their game. I did what I wanted to do and what I thought was better for me and it cost me. You bet it cost me. Would I do it again? You're damn right I'd do it again. But it cost me. I think not making it to the NHL until I was 30, I think I appreciated it more."

Sure, Simmons was thrilled to be on the ice with the best players in the world. But he was also thrilled at what being an NHL goalie could not just do for him, but for those who looked up to him. "To me, sports is all about little kids. And there is nothing like after a game, and you come out and there's some little seven-, eight-year-old kid there with his parents wanting autographs. And to me that was just an awesome thing. That you can kneel down and get at his level and look at him eye to eye and ask him questions [like] do you play hockey, what do you like about it and that."

Simmons's playing days came to an end shortly after this card hit the market. In '78–79 he played in five games for Springfield of the AHL and that was it. L.A. general manager George Maguire sent Simmons to the AHL at the start of the season. Simmons had a bout of pneumonia during training camp and was told to head to Springfield on a five-game stint to get back into shape, with the promise, he says, of a return to L.A. after the five games. "So I went down and played the five games. I told the general manager of the Springfield team, 'Okay, give me a plane ticket back to L.A.' He said, 'Well, I haven't heard from Maguire.' I said, 'Here's what he told me, five games and come back to L.A.' And he said, 'Well, okay.' And I said, 'If he tries to send me back here, I have no desire to play in the minors. I'm 35 years old. So if he tries to send me back here, I'll refuse.' So he said, 'Okay.' I flew back to L.A. and of course Maguire was all upset. 'What the hell are you doing?' And I said, 'You told me five games and I played the five games. Here I am.' It pissed him off big time."

And that was it for the Cobra's playing days. By that time Simmons had already gone into the pizza business with two restaurants, and in a few short years, he and his partners grew their operation into 46 pizza parlors. "It was a license to print money until delivery started."

Eventually the Cobra made it back to the desert. "I always said I'm coming back here. I loved Phoenix. It was Old West, I was Old West." He got heavily involved in the jet-skiing world. The world finals were in Lake Havasu, Arizona, one year. Simmons went and he has basically been there ever since. It's where he gets to see his hockey cards, compliments of fan mail he still receives. "I get them sent [to me]. As a matter of fact I still have 9 or 10 that I just signed that I have to mail back to the people that sent them. Those are the only ones I get."

The Cobra mask didn't travel back to the desert. It is now in the collection of the Hockey Hall of Fame. And yes, sometimes, people still call Gary Simmons "The Cobra." "Hockey people do."

But when he goes back to his hometown, he is not known as the Cobra. "When I go back to Alberta, they call me Moose. That was my name in Lethbridge when I was growing up. My nickname was Moose and the guys that I see up there still call me Moose."

Good thing he was flopping around in the crease one night in Phoenix in 1972. A cobra sure looks a lot cooler on a goalie mask than a moose.

"Yeah, I think so too," he says.

Pat Hickey

LW
221
Height: 5'11" Weight: 180 Shoots: Left
1st Pro Season: 1973-74 Acquired: 1973 Amateur
Draft Born: 5-15-53, Brantford, Ontario
Home: New York, New York

NHL RECORD

YEAR	TEAM	GP	G	A	PTS	PIM
1975-76	RANGERS	70	14	22	36	36
1976-77	RANGERS	80	23	17	40	35
NHL TOTALS	150		37	39	76	71

• Considered to be the fastest skater on the Rangers, he's one of the swiftest men in the NHL. Has excellent balance and the ability to shift and change speeds in an instant on the ice. A versatile type of forward, he's a good two-way player who can also kill a penalty if need be.
• Un des meilleurs patineurs des Rangers, il est l'un des joueurs les plus rapides dans la L.N.H. Son équilibre est excellent et il peut changer de direction ou de vitesse en un instant. Cet ailier gauche est versatile, car son jeu défensif est efficace et il sait gagner du temps durant les pénalités.

Pat drives a black Jeep.
Pat conduit une Jeep noire.

FOR NHL PRODUCTS — © 1977 O-PEE-CHEE PRINTED IN CANADA

PAT HICKEY • L. WING
RANGERS

PAT HICKEY 1977–78 OPC #221

There's cool and then there's New York City cool. And then there's New York City cool in the 1970s: the look, the style, the music, the clubs. We're talking Studio 54. In the late '70s, the New York Rangers were trying a new look, a now classic crest with an angled "RANGERS" under a horizontal "NEW YORK" topped off by a perfect combination of red, white

COOL

and blue. And does anyone look cooler than the smooth skating, on the hustle Pat Hickey on his 1977–78 card?

"It was a pretty good action shot for a bubble gum card. There wasn't a lot of action shots. I'm being chased down," explains Hickey. And he is right. Action shots were still rather uncommon in the era. A typical hockey card featured a simple pose in front of a backdrop.

It only makes sense that Hickey was photographed playing. The guy was a mover and a shaker. He got things done, on the ice—and off.

Over the years I've had the pleasure of interviewing a number of different athletes I used to watch play when I was growing up. At one point in time, I'd tack a card of one of my favourite players on my bedroom wall. It was only a few years later that I ended up interviewing many of those same players. It's one of the things I love about what I do on TV, that link to my youth. I still spend most of my days talking about games. I don't get too starstruck—usually. That is not the case when Pat Hickey reveals who he once was.

First though, a little background. Back in the day, my

brother and I would always get Don Cherry's Rock'Em Sock'Em Hockey videos at Christmas. Watching Don on Christmas was a Reid family tradition. Once in a while though, Santa would stick an extra video in the pile. One year one of those bonus tapes was a hockey bloopers collection. John Davidson was the host. At one point JD introduced a couple of music videos. One of them featured Phil Esposito and a few other Rangers singing "Hockey Sock Rock." Phil was cool. He had the scarf. He had the pipes. For some reason, this song stuck with my brother and me forever. We still sing it every once in a while. When I bring up "Hockey Sock Rock" to Hickey, I am floored.

"That was my deal," says Hickey. But Hickey wasn't in the video. It turns out he was traded to the Los Angeles Kings before Espo, JD, Dave Maloney and Ron Duguay made the famous video. However, Hickey is on the album cover with Phil and the rest of the Rangers Rockers. The night Phil and company made the video, they were down one Rocker.

It gets better. Remember the Rangers' Sasson Jeans ads? Of course you do. Hickey was in on that venture as well.

"I negotiated it. That's a great story."

Details please.

"Long story short, I just had a marketing interest so I spent time in New York with a guy named Sam Silverstein. And that's when merchandise and the proliferation of the t-shirts and everything were going on. So we went to a meeting with a number of clients. But there was a rich guy, Paul somebody, who was starting this designer jeans company, which was the first designer jean company at the time. He had two daughters, so you know me. I wanted to meet the daughters. But anyway, we put this deal together and when the contract finally came out, it was two days of filming and advertising. The original guys were Dugay, Maloney and Davidson. That's who signed up. Phil got wind of this. This was like in June, July, when we put the deal together.

"So this opportunity came up and we signed this deal. And Phil got in it so there was five of us. We did this film for an ad and then we got on a plane and went to Los Angeles and that's when I was traded for [Barry] Beck."

Hickey is quick to give Sonny Werblin credit for the Rangers' late '70s vibe. Werblin ran Madison Square Garden and he got the Rangers out there. Out there as in *everywhere*, and not just in Sasson ads or jiving to the "Hockey Sock Rock." "He ended up taking over the Garden. So he came in and wanted to get to know us and wanted to market us. He put us on *The Dinah Shore Show* and *Merv Griffin Show* and all this kind of stuff."

Hickey still has a few souvenirs of his days with the Rangers, like a "Hockey Sock Rock" album or two. One thing he does not have though is the Jeep. *The Jeep?, you ask?* Flip the card over and there is an awesome cartoon of a hockey player, in full gear behind the wheel of a Jeep with the caption, "Pat drives a black jeep." I love the 1970s. How could a fact like this possibly end up on the back of a hockey card? The '70s were a different decade. And players and the media were just a little closer than they are now. "I used to spend time with writers. I used to drive Frank Brown and Larry Brooks and Laurie Mislin from *Newsday* and Robin Herman from the *New York Times*, who was really the first woman in the locker room, up to practice back in '78, '79 in this black Jeep."

The Jeep, it turns out, was rather handy in the anarchy that is New York City traffic. "When I got down to New York, everybody introduces you to these car dealers and I was driving this Camaro, white Camaro, and I'm not a car guy. Cabbies would run you and sideswipe you and butt in front of you and everything and I said, 'Screw this.' I went back up to Canada, brought my Jeep down with the big bumper and the cabs got out of my way. So somebody from O-Pee-Chee or the press probably wrote that up."

As for the Jeep, it's still out there, likely cruising down an Ontario highway on any given night. "I had that Jeep until probably about five years ago up at the cottage. My wife finally convinced me to get rid of it. And a kid up in Huntsville, he fixed it up, and it's still going."

Hickey had the blond hair, he had the Jeep, he had the Sasson Jeans, and he was a Rangers Rocker. Oh, and did I mention that Hickey used to go to Broadway matinees in the afternoon before Rangers games? "You'd see *Jesus Christ Superstar* and you saw *Man of La Mancha* and *Hair* and all these shows and you'd walk back [to the Southgate Hotel] and maybe get off your feet and have a little cup of tea and some toast. And then you'd go over [to MSG] and entertain 17,500 people. And that's what Sonny Werblin promoted. We were the entertainment. That's sort of like the mantra that it took on. Go out and dance, man. This is New York."

If this card and the story behind it aren't cool, I don't know what is.

DAVE LUMLEY 1980–81 OPC #271

Growing up, my two favourite players were Wayne Gretzky and Guy Lafleur. I also became a big Stéphane Richer fan and was a diehard supporter of fellow Nova Scotian Mike McPhee.

However, at one point in my childhood, pretty much every player in the NHL took a back seat to the man with the curly hair on card number 271 from O-Pee-Chee's 1980–81 set.

For part of my childhood we lived in an old farmhouse. A few times a week, my dad would clear out the kitchen and he and my brother, Peter, and I would play kitchen hockey. During the 1981–82 season, Dad would always ask, "Who wants to be Gretzky and who wants to be Dave Lumley?" We were happy whether we took on the role of No. 99 or No. 20.

"That's really weird," says Lumley when he's told that a couple of brothers in rural Nova Scotia would pretend to be him. "You couldn't have found any other player than me? I can understand the Gretz part about it, but I mean back then we had Messier and Anderson and Kurri and Coffey and Grant Fuhr and you picked me? I don't know whether to be honoured or embarrassed."

Let's go with honoured. Why Lumley? The answer is simple. From November 21, 1981, to December 16, 1981, Dave Lumley went on one of the greatest goal-scoring streaks in NHL history, scoring in 12 straight games. The news of the streak made headlines in the hockey world. My old man obviously picked up on it and informed his hockey-addict sons of Lumley's magic, hence the two kitchen hockey Lumley wannabes.

If you were to go down the Oilers roster and select the player most unlikely to score a goal in 12 straight games, Lumley would be at or near the top of your list during the 1981–82 season. Leading up to the streak, he wasn't scoring. In fact, he wasn't even playing.

"I remember doing a drop pass at the other team's blue line. It got intercepted. The guy went down and scored and I think I sat in the press box for 13 straight games." Benched, Lumley waited for a chance to get back into the lineup. Soon enough a couple of right wingers went down with injuries and Lumley got his chance. Let's rephrase that: Lumley got the opportunity of a lifetime. He wasn't just tossed back into the Oilers' lineup: he became Wayne Gretzky's right winger.

"I asked Jari Kurri, I said, 'What do you do?' He said, 'Assume you're going to get the puck regardless of where Gretz has got it. Just keep your stick on the ice and know where you're going to put it.'" Lumley listened to Kurri's advice as best he could. Then he went to work. It didn't take long for the magic to happen.

"BOOM. Out of nowhere. I remember the first game, I had no goals and no assists going into this game. They put me on Gretz's line. I got a goal, two assists . . . I think I got a couple minutes in penalties and I was plus five. So I erased all the zeroes and put a bunch of ones and twos in the column. Twelve straight!" Lumley is still amazed by what he did all these years later.

Just like that, the relatively unknown guy was suddenly a goal-scoring machine. Of course, if you score 15 goals in 12 games, and you're playing on a line with Wayne Gretzky, you are going to witness some incredible skills. In some cases, the unthinkable and the unimaginable. "I remember one time Gretz going into the corner and I swear to God he looked in the glass. I don't know if he did it or not. I never asked him but it looked like he looked in the glass and saw my reflection and put it on my tape—bang, in the net."

"There are a couple of things I remember. One time in L.A., I don't know why I was on the right point, but the puck was, somebody went to get it out of the end. It was just rolling over the blue line. I just took a wild backhand, kind of a golf shot to keep it in the L.A. end. That thing went straight up in the air, hit the L.A. goalie's back, right in the back of the neck, and went in the net."

"There was another game in Quebec City, I got a penalty shot. I got dragged down. The fact that I got caught from behind isn't a shocker, but anyways, I'm scoring on a penalty shot!"

Everything was working, all the time. Having the greatest playmaker in the history of the game as your centre sure didn't hurt. On the night of December 16, 1981, in Colorado, Lumley needed a goal to keep the streak alive. No. 99 delivered. "We had a four on one. Gretz had the puck and it was Coffey and myself and Kurri. And I hadn't scored that game yet. Gretz looks at Coff, he looks at Kurri, he looks at me, he puts it right on my tape, bang. Extends the streak."

The streak came to an end on December 17th against the Calgary Flames. Lumley had a shadow on him that night. He can't remember the player's name, but all these years later he is still astonished that he had a shadow. "I mean, what's wrong with this picture?" Lumley's goal-scoring streak was over, but he wasn't about to start a slump. The Oilers' next game was at home against Minnesota. Lumley put on another show. "[I] got three goals, three assists and was second star. The little weasel Gretz, I think he got seven points that game [three goals and four assists]. He was first star," says Lumley.

An incredible streak for a guy whose rookie card is most likely buried in commons piles everywhere. It pays to look a little into the history of the guys on your hockey cards, even the cards that aren't worth hundreds of bucks. Even the ones that sometimes aren't even worth a buck.

When Lumley sees his rookie card, he doesn't think much of it. Of course, when others bring it up to him, the streak isn't the first thing they ask about. You know what the first question is when it comes to this card. It's got to be about the hair.

"That's what everybody says to me now: 'What happened to the afro?'" So many people ask me if that was a perm. It was never a perm; I just had long curly hair. That's one of the things people say to me when they see me now, what happened to the big hair? I tell them, 'Well, I'm a grown-up now.' You have to look like a grown-up."

The curly hair from his rookie card may be long gone, but the memories of his streak and his days with the Oilers won't fade away anytime soon. Dave Lumley won two Stanley Cups with the Oilers. And that little 12-game streak put him in a tie for fourth on the list of the NHL's longest consecutive goal-scoring streaks, four behind the record of 16.

"It was magical, I tell you."

Billy Harris

| | Height: 6'2" | Weight: 195 | Shoots: Left |

RW
126

1st Pro Season: 1972-73   Acquired: 1972 Amateur
Draft   Born: 1-29-52, Toronto, Ontario   Home:
Toronto, Ontario

NHL RECORD

YEAR	TEAM	GP	G	A	PTS	PIM
1972-73	ISLANDERS	78	28	22	50	35
1973-74	ISLANDERS	78	23	27	50	34
1974-75	ISLANDERS	80	25	37	62	34
1975-76	ISLANDERS	80	32	38	70	54
1976-77	ISLANDERS	80	24	43	67	44
NHL TOTALS		396	132	167	299	201

• The Islanders' all-time leading scorer, he was the
first player ever drafted by club as amateur. One of
the best two-way players on the club, he has a
current streak of 396 consecutive games played
since entering league.
• Meilleur compteur des Islanders depuis leur
fondation, il fut aussi le premier amateur repêché
par ce club. Un des meilleurs joueurs
offensifs-défensifs de l'équipe, cet ailier droit joua
396 matches consécutifs après son entrée dans la
ligue.

Billy is excellent
on faceoffs.
Billy excelle
à la mise
au jeu.

1977 O-PEE-CHEE PRINTED IN CANADA

BILLY HARRIS • R. WING
ISLANDERS

BILLY HARRIS 1977–78 OPC #126

When it comes to the New York Islanders and classic helmets, Butch Goring gets all the glory. And he does deserve a large chunk of the acclaim; his "Snaps" helmet is legendary. It is either one of the worst helmets of all time or one of the best, depending on your perspective. For me, it's one of the best.

But another Islander deserves some love for his lid. Billy Harris wore an absolute beauty of a dome during his days on Long Island. It's on full display on his 1977–78 O-Pee-Chee.

When you take a good look at the helmet, you almost immediately wonder how old the thing is. What relic of a hockey bag did Harris pull that thing from? It turns out, the helmet was brand new, not an antique at all.

"It was a Cooper helmet, a real fibreglass helmet. It just had that cover on it. It made it look like a real old throwback pic. It was a real helmet."

Yes, it was a legit lid, but it was one different-looking beast. The card demands a double-take thanks to the helmet. The thing looks old, and yes it looks like a throwback, but believe it or not, in the mid- to late '70s, this thing was brand-spanking new. As Harris says, it was not a throwback at all.

He was the only one wearing this type of helmet during the '76–77 season. It was a few years later that a couple of other players tried it out, but at that time Harris was a true original. The lid made its way to the NHL in a roundabout way. Harris says when he turned pro with the Islanders, the only kind of helmet the team had was the "Stan Mikita helmet," the same kind worn by Harris's Islanders teammate Denis Potvin.

During his rookie year, he went *au naturel* and didn't wear a helmet. But during his second year in the league, he decided to try the "Mikita": it did not work for Harris.

"It didn't quite fit and it was really, really heavy. Honest to God, three quarters of the way through the season, you're sitting on the bench and your neck hurt! You know, you could really feel it at the end of a game; your neck was sore from holding the bloody thing up. It was very uncomfortable and very heavy."

So Harris made a call back to Toronto. He dialled up his old buddy Tommy Smythe who ran a sports store in Maple Leaf Gardens. Harris and his sore neck were in need of a new helmet. Harris was on the hunt for an old three-piece lid like the one he wore during his junior days with the Toronto Marlies, but he was out of luck. Smythe didn't have a single one on hand. But . . .

"He said, 'I got some solid blue and solid white, with a sort of leather cover.' But it was a three-piece Cooper helmet. Anyways, the same helmet, it just had that softer leather covering over it. And I said, 'Would you mind sending them down to me, because I have to wear a helmet that is a lot more comfortable and lighter,' and that's where it all evolved from."

It was a move made out of necessity, and it had awesomely stylish consequences. Soon enough the new helmet arrived at the Islanders dressing room, a three-piece lid with that epic leather cover. The helmet looked more than fine and Harris looked more than fine on the ice too. Harris was putting up some solid numbers.

He was an original Islander and he came as advertised. Read the bio notes on the back of the card: "The Islanders' all-time leading scorer, he was the first player ever drafted by the club as an amateur."

The stats don't lie: Harris was solid. At that point in his career, he had put up 299 points in 396 games with the Islanders. Those New York Islanders, a team Billy Harris was a part of from day one, were about to turn a corner. They had Billy Smith in net; Denis Potvin on the point; a young centre named Bryan Trottier; and in the fall of 1977, Mike Bossy joined the team. All the pieces for a great run were falling into place.

Unfortunately for Billy Harris though, on March 10, 1980, just before the Islanders won their first of four straight Stanley Cups, he was traded to the L.A. Kings for the man who many considered to be the final piece of the Islanders Stanley Cup puzzle. Ironically enough, Harris was traded for Butch Goring, the guy with the "Snaps" helmet.

"I just happened to be the sacrificial lamb, getting traded," says Harris. "I was devastated. It was awful. I was there from day one. It was the only team I'd ever played for. We had a lot of lean years. It would have been nice to see the fruits of it."

Harris played until the end of the 1983–84 season with stops in L.A. and Toronto after his days as an Islander. These days he runs a soy-wax candle-making business in the Collingwood, Ontario, area. "We got a hundred stores we supply and we could make it bigger."

As for that old helmet, it made its final hockey card appearance in 1978–79. After that, Harris switched to the "Gretzky JOFA." The whereabouts of Harris's classic lid are unknown. When he retired, he really retired. Harris was living in Los Angeles and hadn't touched the ice in years, nor had he touched his gear. After a few years, he looked at his old mouldy hockey bag on the concrete floor of his garage and decided "to turf it."

Sadly, the epic lid on your old hockey cards is somewhere in hockey helmet heaven right now. However, it turns out hockey card geeks like myself aren't the only ones who remember the old beauty.

"I was playing in Bobby Orr's tournament a couple of summers ago up here in Parry Sound," says Harris, who used to work at Orr's hockey school during his playing days. Sure enough, up came Bobby Orr, with Don Cherry in tow.

"[Bobby] came out and he gives me a big hug. 'Hey, how you doing? How's everything going?' So then he introduced me to Grapes, and Grapes goes, 'I remember Billy for Chrissakes!' and then he makes some comment about my helmet."

KELLY HRUDEY 1986–87 OPC #27

Style is a personal matter. Sure, you can go through life with the same haircut, wearing the same shirt and the same suit. Or you can live a little. Kelly Hrudey chooses to live.

If you've watched *Hockey Night in Canada* over the years, you know that Hrudey knows the game and he knows style. He sports fancy suits that are always on the cutting edge.

Kelly Hrudey was also a rather stylish guy back in his playing days. If you need evidence to back up this argument, just take one look at his 1986–87 O-Pee-Chee. It's glorious: we have a man perm.

"I was getting pressure on the homefront to get the perm," howls Hrudey. "It was in the summer holidays. It was in Edmonton. It was in a place in the West Edmonton Mall.

"Oh my God, that's one of my worst memories from that era . . . that was the time that [it] was kind of cool for guys to get a perm. I didn't pull it off very well."

With all due respect to Hrudey, who tended the NHL twine for 15 seasons, I have to disagree. That is exactly how one should pull off a man perm. As I pointed out to Kelly, sometimes you pay the price for being stylish. You can get pigeon-holed very easily. For example, I was more than proud of my frosted tips and turtlenecked boy-band look circa the year 2000.

"You put that into the perfect perspective, like when you said around 2000, the guys had the frosted tips and all that. And now you look back and you're like, 'Wow, was that ever ugly.' But everybody was doing it," reasons Hrudey. The same thing goes for the man perm.

Of course, Hrudey's style doesn't end with the perm. It is merely the beginning. Supporting the perm, almost as if it is holding it up, is the trademark Hrudey headband. It's the precursor to the full-on bandanna we would soon see in his Los Angeles days. But the headband wasn't just a fashion statement. It came about out of pure necessity.

"I had always had long hair. I had contacts when I played and for anybody out there that wears contacts and sweats a lot, you know that's a bad combo." So along came the headband.

"I ditched that headband from that picture and I went, somewhere right around that time, to a bandanna style, simply because it was more absorbent. And it sort of became a trademark of mine. You can tell that I experimented with a lot of different things." So you may think it was style, but in reality it was a practical move.

Next up, the white gloves. Like a lot of goalies at that time, Hrudey wore a glove on his catching hand to take away the sting of catching shots. As for the glove on his right hand, it was also very necessary.

"In the late '70s, early '80s, there was this thing going around. It was called 'The Gunk.' And guys were getting this rash all over their body," begins Hrudey, who luckily never caught what the hockey world called The Gunk. But around this time, he did get a small rash on his right hand. The glove protected him, along with some medication inside. The Gunk, it seems, is one of hockey's greatest unsolved mysteries.

"It was all associated with sweating and maybe the detergent the teams were using or something. And it was this real odd thing, and nobody really knows, to the best of my recollection, how this thing ever started or why this thing ever went away. But it was a real severe epidemic," recalls Hrudey, who says The Gunk hung around the hockey world for anywhere from five to 10 years.

"There were a few players that ended up having to retire because of this thing. And it was so gross. It was all over their entire body, and it was just gruesome."

If that's not a solid reason to wear a glove on your blocker hand, I don't know what is. So just like the headband, the gloves may look super cool, and super '80s, but they were also super practical. Who knew?

Hrudey, at that time, was in his third full year in the league. He was battling an absolute legend for ice time, Billy Smith. On the ice, Smith was a nasty character, never shy to swipe his stick through the air and down on the ankle of an opponent to clear the front of his crease. "No jobs were given to you," Hrudey explains. "And Billy was awesome for that. If it ever looked like I got on a bit of a roll and maybe to a certain degree [was] getting the upper hand, he'd push back hard—not only in practice but in a really healthy competitive way, he would go fight for his ice time in the coach's room too."

But off the ice, Smith was a really cool dude, says Hrudey. "I found him to be really fun-loving off the ice. It was really cool, because even though we were competing for the same ice time, he and I were almost like the best of friends. We played tennis together off the ice. We had dinner together most nights on the road. We shared a lot of time together, and yeah, there's no question that he was a different person away from the rink. I think to a certain degree he was a little misunderstood. But I always found him to be a pleasure to be around."

As for that perm, like most styles of a certain era, it came and it went. But for a solid five years, that perm was never too far away. In fact, Hrudey saw it every time he crossed an international border. And that happens a lot when you're playing in the NHL. Whenever Kelly Hrudey went through customs, out came the perm.

"That picture you see on that hockey card is not very attractive. But what was worse about that experience is that I also had my passport photo taken at the same time, around the same time I had that perm. And with all due respect to people who have a toupée, but my passport photo clearly looked like I had a toupée sitting on the top of my head. It didn't even look like it was my hair at all. So those two pictures have always stood out to me. That hockey card and then my passport photo."

But at least a passport expires. This hockey card, and that sweet perm that came about in the summer of 1986 at the West Edmonton Mall, will live on in hockey card collections forever.

"You're right. Nobody saw [the passport] but everybody sees that hockey card. Every time somebody shows that to me, I just cringe."

RANDY MOLLER 1991–92 OPC #371

These days Randy Moller is known as one of the most distinctive play-by-play announcers in the National Hockey League, known for his entertaining, over-the-top style.

If you tune into one of Randy Moller's Florida Panthers broadcasts, you're going to get some incredible goal calls. For example, "Rebound! They score! Pour some sugar on me!" That's a little Def Leppard tribute, right there. And Moller quoting Def Leppard is kind of fitting, especially when you look at his '91–92 O-Pee-Chee. Def Lep was on top of the world in the late '80s and early '90s, with their hit songs and sweet hair, and so was Moller—minus the music.

Randy Moller is looking like one cool dude on his '91–92 O-Pee-Chee. He's got the mullet, he's got the chest hair, and he's making his living on Broadway. "I was trying to be like Ron Duguay, I guess. That was my best impression of Ronnie Duguay."

It's not a bad Ron Duguay impression at all. Of course, when you look at Ron Duguay nowadays, he kind of looks the same as he did during his Rangers' days. Moller is the first to admit his look has "changed" over the years. "Obviously [the mullet] was in style at the time, but it's pretty funny looking at it now because if you see me now I don't have much hair left. So there's quite a contrast from that picture to a picture of me now.

"Age does a lot of crazy things to you. It's amazing too, because I seem to be able to grow more hair everywhere else on my body except on top of my head."

Moller, and his now much tamer look, has three kids, all in their 20s. It's a fact: Dad was a cool dude. "My kids really, really, really get a kick out of the [cards] I had with the Rangers when I had the mullet hanging out the back of my helmet . . . they just roll when they see old pictures like that."

Just a few years after this card hit the streets, Moller's career came to an end. He called it quits after playing 17 games with the Florida Panthers in 1994–95. When it was all said and done, he had suited up for an impressive total of 815 regular season games and 78 more in the playoffs. Moller says he retired a little too early, but his retirement from one career led to an opening in another.

"I took a year off and the team [Florida] asked if I wanted to be involved not only doing colour on the radio, but helping to build a brand down here because the team was new." Moller jumped at the opportunity. After a few seasons of doing colour commentary, the Panthers play-by-play position opened up.

"Our president, Michael Yormark, he basically said to me, 'Randy, you're the VP of broadcasting. So you fill the spot, but we'd like you to consider maybe doing play-by-play.' And I took a few days to think about it."

As we know, Moller eventually said yes. Suddenly the guy who grew up listening to Danny Gallivan, Dick Irvin, Bob Cole, Dan Kelly and Rick Jeanneret was now an NHL play-by-play guy.

"It's the greatest decision I've ever made. I really enjoy it. I really, really enjoy it and I never want to do anything else. This is what I want to do and I'm very, very happy about it.

"I'm very, very proud too. I'm humbled to be a part of this fraternity. And I'm also very proud to be the only former player, NHL player, to do play-by-play full time."

As for his play-by-play style, what else did you expect? Take a look at that hockey card again. Randy Moller has style. Randy Moller has charisma. Of course, it has to come through in his broadcasts, in his famous goal calls.

"I played with some characters throughout my career . . . you pick up a lot of your personality from that. And I think once I got into broadcasting, even when I started—when I was doing the colour—I enjoyed that part of it. Letting my personality come out and be entertaining. This is not politics. This is not funeral announcements on your local PBS radio station or whatever. We're here to have fun. As long as you're not disrespecting the sport or the players, have some fun with it. And don't take yourself too seriously."

When Moller travels around North America with the Panthers, his cards pop up everywhere. People are constantly asking him to sign and it's something he is more than happy to do. His old hockey cards are still very special to the man who obviously has a tremendous passion for the game.

"I feel honoured that they're collecting them. You know I'm very proud of those cards. We've kept them, we've kept sets from all of them that I know that exist. We got them here and they'll always be here, and my kids can enjoy them as well. And I feel very, very blessed that there are hockey cards with my pictures and stats on them."

Including the card that shows him starring and styling, in a magical, mulleted role on Broadway.

BILL CLEMENT 1975–76 OPC #189

Thousands if not millions of hockey fans know Bill Clement. His face is beamed into homes across North America. He is one of the game's foremost American voices. Aside from his broadcasting work, he is also a critically acclaimed speaker.

But years ago, once upon a time, when little children

AIRBRUSH

ripped open a pack of hockey cards, this is the Bill Clement they saw. There are few things as awesome (and as disturbing) as Bill Clement's 1975–76 O-Pee-Chee.

It is perhaps both the greatest and worst airbrush job in the history of hockey cards. There is no end to the amount of adjectives you could scribble down on a piece of paper to describe this card, so why not let the man himself, Mr. Clement, take it away?

"I saw some article on the *Bleacher Report*, it was voted one of the worst cards ever," says Clement. And he's just fine with that. "It was awful."

Clement is sporting a huge sweater. This card has a crayon like feel to it. The airbrush job was one of necessity. Following the Flyers' second straight Cup win, Clement was sent to the Washington Capitals. And if you think going from the Stanley Cup champs to an expansion team, which in the previous season set a league record for the fewest wins in a season (eight), is no fun, you would be correct.

"Dog meat" is how Clement describes his Caps team. "I went from the best team in the NHL to the worst team.

"When you win two Stanley Cups, you develop a bond and it's your family. It was as if I was sort of sent out to sea by myself. It was hard. It was as if I was exiled from my family."

And that trade, made in the spring of 1975, set into motion what we are now still in awe of close to 40 years later—Bill Clement's 1975–76 O-Pee-Chee with its giant, crudely drawn sweater, and no space at all between Clement's arm and body. And how about those legs? Someone is in need of a new set of shin pads.

"It looked like I had Eaton's catalogues in my socks." Clement can only imagine the urgency of the card makers, upon hearing that he had been sent to the Caps. "They had no picture of me in a Caps uniform. And the Caps made me captain. And you know, I was like a big deal going to Washington, I mean as big a deal as that could be. And they wanted a card. That's a hand-painted Washington Capitals uniform under me. I can see somebody cutting out a little head of a picture of mine and pasting it on to a storyboard and then whatever technology they had making it work. But it's awful."

Clement says awful; I say, awfully beautiful. Regardless of your take, plenty of people do hold on to this card. When Clement runs into someone tightly holding on to this cardboard treasure, he often offers up this little query. "I ask, 'Do you know who the other guy is in that picture?'"

Take a close look. The guy is rocking your standard '70s haircut. He's a left-handed shot on those "dog meat" Capitals.

"He was not a famous hockey player, but his brother was," continues Clement. "That's Gordie Smith, Billy Smith's brother. So that's the big trivia question I ask people after they finish laughing at the card. I ask them, 'Okay, if you really want to be good at this, who's the guy in the picture with me?' And hardly anyone has ever gotten that."

Clement's time in Washington was short lived. After 46 games in his airbrushed Caps uniform, Clement was sent to Atlanta. The trade to Atlanta was part of a whirlwind three-day adventure, one that comes to mind when Clement reflects back on this airbrushed goody. "I'm also the answer to a dubious trivia question involving Washington. No sooner had that card come out, when I became the answer to this trivia question. 'Who's the only player in NHL history to play three games on three consecutive nights for three different teams in the NHL?'" asks the player turned broadcaster.

The answer, of course, is Clement.

He played in an All-Star Game in Philly on a Monday night. Clement then drove back to Washington and suited up for the Caps the next night. Then, the next day, he was traded to Atlanta. The Flames happened to be in Philly that night, so Clement hopped in his car, drove the three hours to Philly and dressed for this third game, in three different nights, in his third different uniform.

"I don't know how I made it through the third game because I'd been up half the night after the All-Star Game. And then after the game in Washington I didn't get traded [until the next day]. They worked me out. I stayed up late with the guys in Washington. They wanted to hear about the All-Star Game. I hardly had any sleep. Tommy McVie killed us in practice the next day and then said, 'Max McNab wants to see you.' And I get on the phone with Cliff Fletcher [Atlanta's GM] after [Washington] traded me and he says, 'We need you in Philadelphia tonight.' I was like, 'You're bleeping kidding me? I can hardly even lift my arms.' And I went back to Philly and played that night. And we got smoked, I think 7–2, and I slept for a day and a half."

But that 36-hour slumber, and the 36-plus years that followed Clement's trade to Atlanta will never erase the memory of his time in Washington. This airbrushed piece of art ensures that. It ensures that the memory of Clement's time with the Caps will live on forever. "It's one of the ugliest hockey cards ever. And I'm proud to say that I was part of it." Amen.

DENNIS MARUK 1978–79 OPC #141

"The Fu Manchu?" Dennis Maruk asks as our interview begins. Yes, we will get to the Fu Manchu, but first a little background on the man with the Fu.

There are not a lot of players like Dennis Maruk in today's game, but if the game continues to go in the right direction, a few more just might start showing up.

The dead-puck era took players like Maruk out of the game. Why in the world would you want a 5-foot-8, 165-pound sniper, who could seemingly score at will, when you could have a 6-foot-4, 235-pounder who couldn't move? Size meant pretty much everything in the game during the mid- to late 1990s and early 2000s. If a smaller player wanted to make it, chances were he needed to be a pest, not a sniper like Maruk. Luckily the game is moving back towards the more skilled players. See a rather slight Ryan Nugent-Hopkins for evidence.

So let's get to the uber-skilled Dennis Maruk and his '78–79 O-Pee-Chee. Dennis Maruk is a green Washington Capital. Dennis Maruk is a green, airbrushed Washington Capital. Dennis Maruk is a green, airbrushed Washington Capital—with one of the greatest moustaches in NHL history.

The turbulence of the late '70s NHL is responsible for this classic O-Pee-Chee airbrush job. The card is a cavalcade of colours with a fantastically painted green helmet and a brand spanking new painted North Stars jersey. Up in the left-hand corner we get a nice little blue to go with a red banner. And of course the classic O-Pee-Chee "Now with Capitals" is printed on the front.

"When they make that card, you want to make sure that that's the team you're playing for, right? It's kind of funny." Maruk had put the fine folks at O-Pee-Chee into overdrive. Think about what they were up against. A merger between the North Stars and Cleveland Barons sent Maruk to Minny, hence the green airbrush job. But then after just two games with the North Stars, where Maruk says he played one shift, he was traded to the Capitals. Thus the "Now with Capitals" update neatly typed on the bottom-left corner of the card.

From Cleveland to Minnesota to Washington, that's a lot for a player to take—a lot for a card company as well. But the turbulent times were par for the course for Maruk early in his career. Of course, he was in Cleveland after the California Golden Seals moved their franchise from Oakland.

Maruk racked up 94 goals in his first three NHL seasons. He spent year number one in Oakland and years two and three in Cleveland where he was almost a point-a-game player. But these were uncertain times, in terms of both your career and your address. Oakland and Cleveland didn't exactly play in front of sell-out crowds.

"You had to play hard because you knew something was going to happen with the team. In Oakland, Cleveland and then early into Washington, it was kind of 'Oh geez, what's going to happen?' . . . I kept pushing forward. I knew that I had some pretty good seasons. I knew that if I kept playing hard and there was that situation that we were going to a dispersal draft that I'm sure I would have been selected by a number of teams, even a better team."

That's a lot for a young guy to take, but eventually things settled down in Washington. And in 1981–82, everything fell into place. Playing on a line with Ryan Walter and Chris Valentine, Maruk became just the seventh player in NHL history to score 60 goals in a single season. And here's the kicker: his 60 goals were still 32 short of the league lead. "We were all in a different league and then that other guy was in his own league. I think his name was Wayne Gretzky?"

The Great One may have been in his own league, but Maruk was in a pretty amazing league as well when he amassed 60 goals, 76 assists and 136 points. Maruk had finally found a home, just a few years after his epic '78–79 piece of commemorative cardboard.

When you look at the card, it is tough to judge what stands out more: the green airbrush job or the Fu? Let's focus on the Fu.

"A lot of people say it was pretty cool. They say, 'Well, Lanny McDonald had a good 'stache,' and then they see my 'stache and go, 'How come they don't talk about Dennis Maruk's 'stache? That thing was awesome.'"

It turns out we have the world of baseball to thank for Maruk's facial exploits. It all started one day, simply enough, when Maruk was watching a Kansas City Royals game when he saw the hard-throwing Big League pitcher that the baseball world knows as "The Mad Hungarian," sporting a magical, classic 1970s Fu Manchu. At that moment Maruk knew what he had to do. "Al Hrabosky. He had the Fu Manchu and right after that I started the Fu Manchu."

Thank you, Al, and thank you, Dennis.

These days Maruk is a busy man—a busy clean-shaven man. He runs a hockey camp in the summer, plays up to 30 NHL alumni games each winter and dabbles in trade shows.

While the airbrushing of the '70s is a distant memory, the card is a reminder of his two-game stint with the Minnesota North Stars (he would play four-plus seasons in Minny later in his career). Today, the moustache makes an appearance only on Maruk's business cards. "I made up one [business card] like a hockey card, but it's a business card with my Fu Manchu picture and to the right of it is all my info . . . and on the back are all my stats."

And Maruk still pads his stats out on the ice, playing quite a bit. At his weekly Monday skate, Maruk plays with, among others, a wealthy business developer. The man has money. But money can't buy everything. "He comes up every game and he goes, 'I'm pissed at you. I hate you.' And I go, 'Why do you hate me?' And he looks around and he goes, 'Because you've got a hockey card and I don't.' You hear that from a billionaire, a very wealthy man, that's kind of cute."

ROGATIEN VACHON 1971–72 OPC #156

When it comes to hockey cards, the 1971–72 Rogatien Vachon is in a world of its own. It has been picked on, blogged about and stared at for years. In fact, it could be the world's first documented case of "cut and paste." Or perhaps more accurately "how not to cut and paste."

Take a gander. That is clearly Vachon's face. It's his smile, his haircut. But make no mistake: that is not Vachon's body. Not even close. The complexion alone gives that away. At least Vachon ended up with some pretty sweet chest hair as part of the deal.

"Yeah I've seen that card," chuckles Vachon. "I guess they didn't have a very good budget that year.

"I was totally surprised when I saw it too. I think they just pasted my head on a Kings jersey or something. I don't know what happened . . . I thought it was pretty stupid to make a card like this, you know. Who knows, maybe it's worth a lot of money now?"

Well, you won't be putting your kid through college with the '71–72 Vachon, but to some collectors it is priceless.

Flip the card over and you'll discover why the card makers were forced to take desperate measures. They needed Vachon in the gold and purple of the L.A. Kings as soon as possible. The back of the card reads, "A twist of fate sent Roggie to Los Angeles Kings early this season in a trade with Canadiens. Vachon led the Canadiens to a Stanley Cup in 1969 with some hot goaltending. Last season, another hot netminder, Ken Dryden, did the same thing for the Canadiens, relegating Roggie to backup man . . ."

The spring of 1971 was a magical time in Montreal. Ken Dryden came out of nowhere and led the Canadiens to a shocking Stanley Cup win. But as the back of Vachon's '71–72 states, Dryden's heroics did cost Vachon his starting gig in Montreal. This is something that Vachon recalls all these years later when talking about his '71–72 O-Pee-Chee.

"It was pretty simple. Ken Dryden comes in at the end of the year before and he wins a Stanley Cup in '71 and he's the MVP of the playoffs. So at that time we started the season the year after, I think Phil Myre was there, he was the third goalie, so it was pretty crowded. So I went to see Sam Pollock and I asked him if Dryden's gonna play most of the games and he goes, 'Well, I don't think we have any choice, the guy just won the MVP of the playoffs.' So I said, 'Okay, I'm still young. I want to be the number one goalie somewhere.' A little while after I got traded to L.A."

And that was the trade that forced the fine folks at O-Pee-Chee to spring into action. Purple Kings lettering. Yellow background. Rogie Vachon's smiling face and clearly somebody else's body.

"I don't know whose body it was," Vachon says. "The body was a little bigger than mine." Most hockey card geeks, however, have concluded that it is the late Ross Lonsberry's body on the card. Ross provided the body, Rogie the head. It is lovely. And it kicked off Vachon's California adventure.

"That was a real culture shock, let me tell you. I was in Montreal; we won three cups in four and a half years when I was there. And we came into L.A. and our team was really lousy; it was terrible. That same year I popped my knee and I was out for the rest of the year so I missed most of the '71–72 season and I think they were pretty much out of the playoffs by Christmas."

Vachon could go anywhere in L.A. He could do anything. Members of the L.A. Kings were free to roam the streets at anytime. No one stopped you and asked for an autograph. L.A. was no Montreal. But that all changed, Vachon says, in 1974–75 when the Kings, led by Marcel Dionne up front and Rogie Vachon in goal, had a 105-point season. It's a franchise record that still stands.

"That whole thing changed in 1974–75 when we started putting some good numbers on the ice and we were competing with all the top teams and all the fans started to come to the games," recalls the former 'tender.

Vachon found his stride. He was the runner-up for the Hart Trophy in '74–75. In the fall of 1976, he led Team Canada, a team that some regard as the greatest collection of players ever, to a Canada Cup title. The Kings retired his No. 30 in 1985.

Vachon had all that success because he asked the Habs for a trade. That's the story behind this classic airbrush cut-and-paste '71–72 Vachon.

"If I would have stayed in Montreal, even though I would have played 20 games a year, I would have won a lot of cups . . . at the same time, I just wanted to play. I could have stayed on the bench and watched Ken Dryden play, but I didn't want to do that," says Vachon.

And that is a good thing. That is, after all, why we have this classic card. Vachon still sees it all the time, 40-plus years after kids first ripped it out of a pack, wondering why in the world the head didn't seem to fit that body.

"I see it all the time because I still get a lot of fan mail . . . Everytime I sit down and answer my mail, that card is always creeping up. And I always laugh when I see it."

I get a chuckle out of it too, Rogie. It's nice to know that one of the greatest goalies to ever play the game, a three-time All-Star, also has an all-star sense of humour.

MIKE EAVES 1983–84 OPC #79

Mike Eaves looks all business on his '83–84 O-Pee-Chee. His helmet's on, but it's not too tight. His chinstrap is undone; you have to keep it cool after all. He has that classic '80s look—the 'stache, the curly hair and yes, the airbrushed touch-ups. Having a crudely drawn uniform pasted over your body was not a big deal back in the day, according to Eaves. But he did notice the airbrushing right from the start.

"It looked a little different than the other ones, because you can tell that it's been doctored up a little bit . . . it's an airbrush, I guess. I knew it looked a little different than the other ones just because of that fact. So it stands out a little bit more," says Eaves, now the head coach of the Wisconsin Badgers. "I had the big hair back then, little moustache going. It's funny when you're younger, you want to look older so you grow some facial hair and then when you're older, you want to look younger so you shave it off."

As in most cases, it was a trade that forced the airbrushing: Eaves was sent to Calgary from the Minnesota North Stars in a four-player deal in June 1983. "Going back to Calgary was interesting, because it's actually where my roots are. My mom and dad were born and raised there, so it was in some fashion going back to family. Aunts and uncles and stuff like that. My grandparents were there when they were alive so that was interesting."

The deal also reunited Eaves with his old college coach, the legendary "Badger" Bob Johnson. Eaves played for Johnson at Wisconsin during his college career in the '70s.

"Bob knew what I was capable of doing and he wanted to give me an opportunity to be a part of what he was doing up there; he figured I would understand what he was trying to get done so it was good on many fronts," says Eaves.

And Johnson did know what he was doing. He led the Flames to the 1986 Stanley Cup Final against Montreal. The Canadiens won the series in five games. And that was it for Mike Eaves. Eaves missed the entire

'85–86 regular season. He played eight games in the playoffs. Then he retired at the age of 28.

Concussions put an end to his playing days.

His second life in the game began as a coach. He was put on Johnson's staff for the following season. "An assistant assistant coach" is how Eaves sums up his first coaching job with the Calgary Flames. "That was my foot in the door as far as getting on to my next step and my next career."

Would Eaves have ever eased that easily into coaching without the deal that sent him to Calgary? "I don't think so. I think because Bob again knew who I was, the type of person I was, and having that relationship, I think he was comfortable with me being around in the coaching room and those types of things. It certainly did help."

Eaves's coaching career has taken him to Philly, Finland, Pittsburgh, Hershey, a stint with the U.S. National Junior program and other stops in between. Finally, starting with the 2002–03 season, Eaves wound up back in Madison, Wisconsin, as the head coach of Badger Bob's old team, the Wisconsin Badgers.

"We were fortunate to have a lot of good jobs along the way and stay in the business . . . My wife put it best, she's from Madison, and we must have moved almost 20 times before we came back to Madison and she said, 'You know what? The circus has finally come home.'"

Eaves comes across that old airbrushed piece of cardboard all the time. The card pops up in his fan mail. His two sons, Patrick and Ben, who have gone on to pro careers, used to come across their dad's old cards all the time, even the '83–84 O-Pee-Chee.

"When they were in their teenage years, they'd say, 'So Dad, what's that worth now, like 25 cents?'" says Eaves. "And at the time because they were so young, I could say, 'Well, at least I got one.' But now I can't say that anymore, because Pat's got some and I think Ben has a couple as well."

But surely none as sweet as the old man's '83–84 O-Pee-Chee.

Considered to be one of the top young defensemen in pro hockey ranks, Bryan came to the Stingers in an off-season trade with the Crusaders. His 6'3" frame and 210 lb. playing weight makes him the biggest of the Cincinnati defensive corps. Played junior hockey for Medicine Hat.

54 BRYAN MAXWELL

SHOOTS: LEFT HEIGHT: 6'3" WEIGHT: 210
BORN: 9-7-55. LETHBRIDGE. ONT.

Career Statistics		Statistiques de carrière			
	GAMES	GOALS	ASSISTS	TOT. PTS.	PEN. MINS.
1975-76	73	3	14	17	177
LIFETIME	73	3	14	17	177

Considéré comme l'un des meilleurs jeunes défenseurs dans le hockey professionnel. Bryan fut échangé par les Crusaders entre les saisons. Ce gars de 6'3" et 210 livres est le plus robuste défenseur des Stingers. Bryan a joué pour le club junior de Medicine Hat.

© O-PEE-CHEE PRINTED IN CANADA.

DEFENSE

BRYAN MAXWELL
STINGERS

Stingers

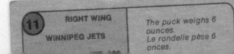

BRYAN MAXWELL 1976–77 OPC #54 (WHA)

I have always been fascinated with the WHA, though I can't remember watching the games. Maybe it was because an old friend of the family used to work the lines in the league. Maybe it's because I've always been a fan of '70s fashion. Maybe it's because as a hockey nerd, the WHA produced so many stories and had such a huge effect on the game in such a short amount of time. It's likely a combination of all of the above. Based on what I've read, watched and been told, the final couple of WHA seasons were crazy times. Teams were on the move, addresses were changing and players were caught in the middle of it all. It was a case of permanent flux.

And that, of course, meant that card makers had to be on their toes. Keeping track of the whereabouts of players was no easy task. Think about it. Everyone's go-to reference, HockeyDb.com, was still decades away.

But there were positives. The turbulence and the chaos of the WHA brought us this fine piece of cardboard—Bryan Maxwell's rookie card.

This is not just any rookie card. Sure, it's your run-of-the-mill WHA pose shot. But then the airbrushing takes over. It's a Cincinnati Stingers card, but as you can plainly see, the airbrush doctor made no attempt to draw the Stingers' logo. They didn't even bother trying to colour the thing black and gold. It resembles a simple white sheet, draped over the body of an unsuspecting player. Few players, I am sure, would like to be airbrushed on their first ever hockey card. But it's not the doctoring that Maxwell talks about all these years later.

"That's not even me," says Bryan Maxwell. That's the kicker. The airbrush, maybe you can live with that, but a case of mistaken identity combined with an airbrush job on your first card? Now that's a double whammy.

So, of course, after all these years, there's no mystery as to who the man on the card is . . . right?

"I don't know who it is on my Cincinnati card," says the former player turned coach turned businessman, who runs a shuttle service,

ShuttleMax, between Lethbridge and Calgary. His reaction upon seeing the card now is the same one he had the first time he saw it decades ago: "Holy geez! Who the heck is this?"

Maxwell's rookie card started a trend as far as his cardboard went. It seems he was one tough guy to identify. He was a journeyman on the ice. In the '76–77 season, he played for the WHA Stingers and the American League's Springfield Indians. The following season he suited up for three teams: Minnesota in the NHL, the Binghamton Dusters of the AHL and the WHA's New England Whalers.

Apparently all that moving and shuffling around created more confusion. Maxwell didn't have a card for the '77–78 season, but when '78–79 rolled around there was more trouble. His second-ever hockey card was much like his first one.

"On my North Stars card, it's Brad Maxwell on the front—it's not me. It's Brad. And then it's my information on the back," says a baffled Maxwell. Two cards, two different people, neither the intended target. Bryan Maxwell's hockey card career was off to a tough start. He was 0-for-2.

You can see how a card company could make the mix-up, can't you? There were two Maxwells in the game with the same initials, BM. But come on, there was one obvious hint as to who was who. "He's a right-handed shot and I'm a lefty."

Perhaps the card companies had had enough of Bryan Maxwell. They gave him another couple of years off. After stops in Oklahoma City, St. Louis and Salt Lake, Maxwell wound up in Winnipeg for the 1981–82 season.

With his time in Winnipeg came the third and final hockey card of his NHL career. The only question, would it truly be a Bryan Maxwell hockey card? The player who began his pro career with the WHA's Cleveland Crusaders in '75–76 surely had done enough after all these years to warrant his own face on his own hockey card.

When kids ripped open a pack of cards in 1982–83, it was justice for Bryan Maxwell. Finally, Bryan Maxwell was on a Bryan Maxwell hockey card.

"The only card that's me is the Winnipeg Jets card. The one with just my head."

Looking back all these years later, Maxwell says it's no great tragedy that he was only on one of his three hockey cards, it would have been a bit of a bonus though. "It would have been nice now, especially getting older and stuff, to have those as keepsakes, for sure." But Maxwell did end up getting a good story out of the deal. And yes, he did end up getting his own picture on his own hockey card. Granted, it took three tries.

Maxwell sees "his" old cards all the time. The mystery of just who is on his rookie card lives on. The Brad and Bryan confusion lives on. He gets his airbrushed error and the North Stars error in the mail all the time. "I don't sign them. Just because they're not me," says the man who spent years in the coaching ranks once his playing days came to an end.

So if you ever get the urge to send Maxwell a card in the mail, make sure he's in a Jets uniform. And if you do know how Maxwell went 1-for-3 in his card career, please let him know. After all these years, the cause of the confusion, the reason as to why he's only on one of his three hockey cards, is still a mystery to him.

C/LW

MIKE KRUSHELNYSKI

KINGS

O-Pee-Chee

"Traded to Kings 8-9-88"

221 MIKE KRUSHELNYSKI

LW/AG · EDMONTON OILERS

HEIGHT: 6'2"   WEIGHT: 200   SHOOTS: LEFT
Last Amateur Club: Montreal Juniors (79-80)
Acquired: Trade with Boston (6-21-84)
Born: 4-27-60, Montreal, Que.   Home: Montreal, Que.

NHL RECORD/FICHE DANS LA LNH

Year Année	Team Équipe	GP	G	A	PTS	PIM
81-82	BRUINS	17	3	3	6	2
82-83	BRUINS	79	23	42	65	43
83-84	BRUINS	66	25	20	45	55
84-85	OILERS	80	43	45	88	60
85-86	OILERS	54	16	24	40	22
86-87	OILERS	80	16	35	51	67
87-88	OILERS	76	20	27	47	64
NHL Totals/Totaux dans la LNH		452	146	196	342	313

GAME WINNING GOALS/BUTS GAGNANTS 1987-88: 0

PLAYOFF RECORD/FICHE DURANT LES ÉLIMINATOIRES

	GP	G	A	PTS	PIM
1988	19	4	6	10	12
Career/Carrière	88	24	29	53	82

NATIONAL HOCKEY LEAGUE LIGUE NATIONALE DE HOCKEY

OFFICIAL LICENSED PRODUCT PRODUIT LICENCIÉ OFFICIEL

© 1988 NHLPA

©1988 O-PEE-CHEE CO. LTD.

NHLPA

PTD. IN CANADA/ IMPRIMÉ AU CANADA

MIKE KRUSHELNYSKI 1988–89 OPC #221

If airbrushing was an art, the '88–89 Mike Krushelnyski may just be the masterpiece. By the late '80s, airbrushing was very much a part of the sports card world. There were still all kinds of horrors in every kid's collection, but at least with the Krushelnyski there was a little flair.

You can see the shadows drawn on the uniform. There's even an effort to make for a little glare from the lights on Krushelnyski's CCM helmet. And when you think about it, this card deserved a little extra attention. Just about every airbrushed card is the result of a trade. This card exists because of *the* trade.

The date is right there—it's like Krushelnyski is staring at the date that changed hockey forever. August 9, 1988. The day Peter Pocklington traded (some say sold) Wayne Gretzky to the L.A. Kings. Krushelnyski and Marty McSorley were the other two Oilers involved in the deal.

In fact August 9, 1988, could be considered the day I began my career as a sportscaster, and I have Krushelnyski, in part, to thank. I'll never forget the day: it was hot, extremely hot. So, of course, like your typical nerd, I was inside watching TV. And that's when it happened.

A news update from Detroit's CBS affiliate flashed across the screen (don't ask me why Pictou, Nova Scotia, got its CBS feed from Detroit). Sportscaster Eli Zarret delivered the news: Wayne Gretzky had been traded to the L.A. Kings.

I don't know why, but I felt the need to tell the world about this deal. I ran outside and found my SuperCycle. I was headed to where the kids were. I pumped my legs as hard as I could. The world at that time revolved around the Pictou tennis courts. On my way there, I saw my brother and I pedalled towards him; out of breath, I yelled, "Gretzky's been traded!" He was in shock. We made our way to the tennis courts where we broadcasted the news. It seemed like the whole world had stopped, when I look back on it. Most of the kids probably just shrugged, but I do remember a few who were almost as shocked as my brother and I were. It was a monumental moment in my childhood.

If this was a big deal for me, what about for Krushelnyksi? What did this deal mean to his career? And what about his hockey card that went from an Oilers uniform to a painted version of the Kings' threads?

"I think it's excellent," says Krushelnyski. "I think the first time I ever saw it was when someone came up and asked me to autograph it. I'm like, 'Oh man, look at this. What the heck is this?' It's all airbrushed, so it's just hilarious."

That trade, forever immortalized on this card, changed the game of hockey. It was suddenly on the front page of every newspaper in America. Krushelnyski and the Oilers were fresh off a Cup win. He didn't see it coming. And like just about everyone else on the planet, he never thought the Oilers would trade No. 99, even after the rumours had begun to swirl in the summer of 1988.

"I was running a hockey school in the Eastern Townships and reporters were all around for the last three days. And I was like, 'Boys, it's only a hockey school. What are you . . .'"

Before the man who played four seasons in Edmonton could utter another word, that gaggle of reporters interrupted him. They weren't interested in a hockey school. They wanted to know about all these Gretzky rumours. Could the Great One be on his way out of Edmonton?

"I'm like, 'They're never going to trade Gretzky. He's Canada. There's the '72 Series, Paul Henderson and Gretz.' You can't get any bigger than that. Three days later, what do I know? We were off to L.A."

It happened. We all know the scene: Molson House in Edmonton. That famous Gretzky press conference, when he had to say goodbye to the Oilers. Krushelnyski had to say goodbye too.

"I got wind about one o'clock and they say, 'Listen, you've been involved in a trade but we can't release the details yet, 'cause we're still looking for one more party.' It was McSorley, who was in the Maritimes running a hockey school or something. And I think they announced the trade an hour later. So I really don't know how Marty found out."

As soon as things were official, Krushelnyski did what any good hockey player would do. He looked for a Kings' roster. He wanted to size up his new team's chances. He liked what he saw. Then hockey went Hollywood. As far as Krushelnyski is concerned, it was Hollywood right off the bat.

Athletes—check. Movie stars—check. Rock stars—check. Welcome to Los Angeles.

"It was great. Bruce McNall [the Kings' owner] had us going to black tie affairs every 10 days. It was wonderful. We got to meet Hollywood people and they got to meet us." They even met a couple of athletes who themselves had gone Hollywood. One of them was a rather notorious football player turned actor turned . . . "I got a picture with Dick Butkus, you know, and O.J. Simpson—before the glove," says Krushelnyski.

There were rock stars too. After a game one night, Krushelnyski hit the showers. When he emerged from his post-game cool down, wearing only a towel, he stumbled into one of the biggest rock stars of all time. "Bruce Springsteen. How cool is that, eh?" Somewhere in the Krushelnyski collection there is a picture of the Boss and the Krush, clad in just a towel.

And then there was the great John Candy. He had bought the CFL's Toronto Argonauts with Gretzky and McNall. One summer day, Krushelnyski found himself at an Argos game. And, what do you know, in strolled the legendary Canadian actor.

"We're sitting in the box and John Candy comes in running—'Krusher, how are ya!' And he's hugging me. My wife said, 'What the heck are you doing? How do you know this guy?' Man, that guy was more excited to see me than the game. I thought, 'You gotta be kidding me!' He's hugging me? It was so awesome."

The Kings were a solid team on the ice too. During Krushelnyski's two playoff runs with L.A. they ran into the defending Stanley Cup Champions on two occasions. The Kings beat the Oilers in the spring of 1989. They took out the Flames in the spring of 1990. (Krushelnyski scored the series winner against the Flames in double overtime.) Hollywood was in love with hockey, even though the Kings never went all the way to win a Stanley Cup.

"It was just phenomenal. We just ran out of gas."

After 15 games with the Kings in the 1990–91 season, Krushelnyski was traded to the Toronto Maple Leafs. His time in Hollywood had come to an end. It all started on that famous date, typed across his airbrushed 1988–89 O-Pee-Chee: "Traded to Kings 8-9-88." It's a date hockey fans will never forget. It's a date Mike Krushelnyski will never forget. It started his Hollywood adventure. All those memories come rushing back, courtesy of one chat about his airbrushed '88–89 O-Pee-Chee.

"Can you imagine one card, what a conversation!"

Ken Linseman 1984–85 OPC #7

At first glance, Ken Linseman's 1984–85 O-Pee-Chee doesn't seem all that remarkable. It's a nice action shot of Linseman, head up and in the play. Look a little closer though and an amazing story begins to emerge.

That's Ken Linseman all right, at least part of him.

"As the season started and the first person asked me to sign it, I'm looking at it and something seems weird here. I'm definitely not this tall," says Linseman, who is listed at 5-foot-10 on the back of the card. And the closer Linseman looked, he came to realize the obvious explanation for his sudden growth spurt. It was his head all right—perched right on top of Mike Krushelnyski's body. The 5-foot-10 Linseman was suddenly 6-foot-2.

"You keep looking closely at the card, they pretty much, I think, just put my head and helmet on and everything else is Mike," says Linseman all these years later.

Who do we have to thank for this beauty of a hockey card? Well, a few people. Let's start with the card makers who airbrushed their best Linseman-Krushelnyski hybrid. And we also have to thank one of the greatest hockey players of all time, Mark Messier.

This is how the story goes. In the spring of 1984, 25-year-old Ken Linseman had an amazing playoff run with the Edmonton Oilers. Linseman had the series-clinching goal in the three-of-four series win as the Oilers went on to win their first Stanley Cup. Not bad for a guy who didn't really have a regular line during the Oilers playoff run. Linseman, a centre, describes himself as "a rover" during that 1984 Cup run.

How did Linseman end up as a rover? The answer is simple: Mark Messier. When Linseman went down with a knee injury in the '84 season, the Oilers moved Mark Messier into Linseman's centre spot on the team's second line. When Linseman returned to the Oilers lineup, he was all over the place. He was racking up goals, 10 of them in the playoffs, while doing spot duty with a number of different linemates. After the Oilers won the Cup, Linseman knew his time in Alberta was coming to an end, despite his outstanding playoff run.

"As soon as Mark moved to centre, I knew I had to go, 'cause you certainly weren't going to move either of those guys [Gretzky and Messier], and you just can't have three offensive centres," says Linseman.

So on June 21, 1984, the Edmonton Oilers sent Ken Linseman to the Boston Bruins straight up for Mike Krushelnyksi. A few months later, one magical hockey card hit the corner stores.

"It really stood out to me. I thought, 'There's no way my legs are that long,'" says Linseman of that '84–85 O-Pee-Chee. Linseman may have looked a little strange on the front of that card, but he fit in very nicely at the Boston Garden, centering Barry Pederson and the fantastically skilled Rick Middleton.

Linseman spent the next five and a half seasons in Boston. He even made a final cameo in Edmonton, playing 56 games with the Oilers in 1990–91 before wrapping up his career with two games as a Toronto Maple Leaf in 1991–92. Mike Krushelnyski, he of the lower body, played in 72 games for those '91–92 Leafs, but the topic of the card didn't come up until they teamed up as old-timers.

"We were playing hockey up in Canada together. It was the Bruins alumni, and the card came across the table for me to sign. And I said, 'Well, I'll sign here by my head if you go get him [Krushelnyski] to sign by the body.'

"At that point, I yelled over to him about it all. He would never have seen the card, because it was my name and my head and stats," recalls the man who started his career with the infamous Birmingham "Baby" Bulls in the WHA back in 1977–78.

Yes, the card features Linseman's name, Linseman's head and Linseman's stats. But one question remains thanks to some 1980s fashion. Take a look at the front of this card once again. Do you see that awesome Bruins V-neck collar that Linseman (or Krushelnyski) is sporting? No laces at the top. No circular collar. No, we are given the gift of the V-neck. Which, in turn, gives us the gift of chest hair. Linseman can verify that those are not his arms, that's not his No. 25 and those are

definitely not his legs. However, he is stumped by that clump of chest hair protruding from the black and gold Bruins uniform. "It could be my hair . . . I don't know where they cut it off. Because I definitely had hair coming out of my chest," says Linseman.

But here comes the confusion. If you look at any Krushelnyski card, you can make the same argument about the chest hair. Conclusion: some mysteries are better left unsolved.

As for what a Linseman-Krushelnyski hybrid type player would look like on the ice, the man known as "The Rat" can only imagine.

"I guess I ended up better because I got his body, right? It would have been nice to have his body, but if I had his body I might not have had my tenacity," says Linseman, who racked up 807 points and 1,727 PIMS in his NHL career. "Could you imagine Mario Lemieux with all that tenacity? Most big guys aren't very mean."

Linseman only sees his 1984–85 O-Pee-Chee when he signs it, though he figures he may still have a few around his house somewhere. He spends his time in real estate and surfing. And all these years later, the card, and that he and Krushelnyski got a chance to have a chuckle over it, still makes him laugh. "[The card] was just funny. And it just was funny that we were in the same place at one point where we got to talk about it."

As for who got the better deal on the card, Linseman figures he benefitted the most from this mid-'80s airbrush job.

"Well, I'm definitely better looking than him, make sure you pass that on."

CHUCK LUKSA • D

HARTFORD WHALERS

370

CHUCK LUKSA D WHALERS

Playing Record • Fiche comme joueur

HEIGHT: 6'1". WEIGHT: 197
SHOTS: Left
1st PRO SEASON: 1974-75
ACQ: Trade with Cincinnati
BORN: 7-15-54, Toronto, Ontario
HOME: Toronto, Ontario

	GP	G	A	PTS	PIM
1978-79	78	8	12	20	116
Lifetime • Carrière	78	8	12	20	116

A solid defenseman, Chuck is a bruiser known for his tenacious checking on ice. • Ce défenseur robuste est reconnu
pour sa mise en échec tenace.

Chuck played on 2 Nova
Scotia Calder Cup teams.
Chuck aida 2 fois la
Nouvelle-Écosse à
gagner la
Coupe Calder.

© 1979 O-PEE-CHEE PRINTED IN CANADA

Look for
NHL Products
Recherchez
les produits
de la LNH

Chuck Luksa 1979–80 OPC #370

When you call someone about their one and only hockey card, you never know what you are going to talk about: their one moment in the "show," what could have been or what never was? Eternal gratitude or eternal bitterness? When I got a hold of Chuck Luksa, we ended up talking about a baby shower.

I HAD A CARD — Chapter Seven

Chuck Luksa's NHL career lasted eight games. He had one assist for one point to go along with four minutes in penalties for the 1979–80 Hartford Whalers. He played a total of nine pro seasons; he won two Calder Cups with the Nova Scotia Voyageurs, but only had one legit O-Pee-Chee hockey card.

"What was it like having a hockey card? It would have been better having a longer career in the NHL. But having a hockey card was fine," says Luksa, who entered the real estate game in the Toronto area once his playing days came to an end.

"When the hockey card was made, I had people coming to me [to] sign the thing, giving them to me. I had about 25 of them over the years. I did some speaking in those early years or whatever, and I'd give the cards away. I'd sign them and give them away. Turned out about 10 years ago, I didn't have any left for myself. I was all out, but I've got a couple now. People have kindly bought them, spent their 25 cents—I think they're worth about [that now], something like that. It would have been nicer to play longer."

Based on the stats on the back of his card, I'm sure the card makers thought Luksa was going to play a prominent role in Hartford's first NHL season. He played in 78 games the year before with Cincinnati, a team that boasted a young Mark Messier. Following the '78–79 season, the Whalers picked up Luksa. Obviously that meant he'd get to play with Gordie Howe, but he didn't go into Hartford's room in childlike awe of Mr. Hockey. In fact he had to keep his head down, kind of hoping he wouldn't get noticed. In the '78–79 season, Luksa scored two goals in a Cincinnati win over Hartford. No big problem. The problem was, during that same game, he and Mr. Hockey had come into "contact" with one another.

"I happened to hip-check Gordie. He was coming down the boards. And Gordie ended up going over the boards into his bench when I hip-checked him. He sort of went over the boards on his back and landed in the laps of the guys sitting on the bench, and they threw him back out. And of course he came at me. I didn't mean to put him out of the rink. It just happened."

So now you've got a problem. It's right there in Luksa's own words: "He came at me." You've just hip-checked one of the greatest players of all time. And even at the age of 50, he is still Gordie Howe. What do you do if you're 24-year-old Chuck Luksa?

"I had bumped my rear end against the boards. I went down and I was just getting back up and he took a swing at me and he nailed me. Nailed me with a glove. His glove was on his hand. He didn't drop his glove and he followed through with his elbow."

Chuck Luksa took a famous Gordie Howe elbow right in the face. So now, again, what do you do if you're 24-year-old Chuck Luksa?

"I just remember thinking, 'Okay, what am I going to do here? If I drop the gloves I'm fighting Gordie Howe and [if] I win they're going to say I beat up an old man, because he *was* old at the time. And if I drop the gloves and lose, they're going to say I got beat up by an old man.' And I thought, 'You know what—I can't win this. No matter which way it goes I'm gone.' So I just went back into the play." A fantastic decision that Luksa just looks back on now with laughter. It could have been really painful back in the winter of 1978–79 though.

So let's get back to Luksa strolling into that Hartford room. What did he do? Did he go up and apologize profusely for hip-checking one of the greatest players to ever play the game? Did he go up and tell Gordie that he would bring that same fire to his Whalers? Nope, it turns out that he didn't say a thing.

"Never ever said a word," says Luksa.

So what does any of this have to do with a baby shower? The answer unfortunately cannot be found on the back of a hockey card. Luksa only played eight games for the Whalers. He ended up playing 72 games for Springfield of the AHL during the 1979–80 season. One of Luksa's teammates there was Marty Howe.

"We had our first child that year and Marty and his wife held a shower for us." And guess who came to the shower? Gordie and Coleen Howe. It gets better: Chuck's mom and dad were in town, the same dad that used to take Chuck to Maple Leaf Gardens when he was a kid.

"It's one of those interesting things. I mean my father, going way back, and I don't know what it would be the late '50s or early '60s, went down and watched the Leafs play. And I remember him taking me occasionally on his shoulders because I was just a young little kid. At that point in time, they could take a kid in on their shoulders, and I recall seeing Gordie Howe when [the Leafs] played against the Wings. And here we were how many years later? And Gordie and Colleen came, and my parents just happened to be down at that time visiting us. And so they were there as well. And Gordie, what a gentleman he was. He sat on the chesterfield, talked with my father for about two and a half hours."

I can't think of a better way to repay your old man for taking you on his shoulders to all those Leafs games. "It's got nothing to do with hockey. It's got everything to do with the individual that Gordie is—a good, good man," Luksa says.

It's too bad Luksa only had one card. If he'd had one the year before, maybe Gordie could have avoided the hit. After all, the scouting report for Luksa is right there on the back of the card: "A solid defenseman, Chuck is a bruiser known for his tenacious checking on ice."

BILL ARMSTRONG 1991–92 OPC #36

Bill Armstrong makes his living as a real estate agent in London, Ontario. But once upon a time, Bill Armstrong, real estate agent, was Bill Armstrong, hockey prospect. He has the hockey card to prove it.

The folks at O-Pee-Chee and Topps thought enough about the 25-year-old to include him in their '91–92 set even though he only had one game of NHL experience. He was listed on his card as a "Top Prospect."

"It was pretty neat," recalls Armstrong. "I mean when you're coming up and obviously trying to crack the big lineup, the big team, that's obviously something that comes along with that. And it kind of surprised me, because nobody told me that the card was going to be made. All of a sudden it just showed up."

The card makers thought big things were in store for Armstrong, and so did he. The NHL stats on the back of his card read one game played, no goals, one assist, one point. They would stay that way forever. Armstrong suited up for the Flyers once in 1990–91. And that was it. He would never play in the NHL again.

"I get this all the time when people ask me about my card. They'd say, 'One game? Is that all you played?' Well, they don't see the miles that you put on being called up and sent down. And in those days, you'd get called up 10 or 15 times and never get to play a game. You just sit in the press box. So they don't get the full story of what went on or how many exhibition games you played with that team or how much work you did with that team."

Hockey is a funny game; one minute you're a "Top Prospect" and then not so much anymore. Bobby Clarke signed Armstrong out of college. Unfortunately for Armstrong, and Clarke, the Flyers gave Clarke the boot shortly after Armstrong signed. Russ Farwell was hired as the Flyers new general manager. Armstrong says he just simply wasn't his guy. "You know what happens when GMs come in. They bring in the guys they know and they trust. He was from out west. He was from the WHL, so he started bringing in a bunch of WHL people. And I kind of started to slide out of favour just because he didn't know me."

Bill Armstrong went on to a lengthy minor league career. Some of the numbers he put up were absolutely astounding. In the mid-1990s he spent his time in the IHL and the AHL. He had four straight seasons where he scored over 30 goals. He was racking up the points, but for some reason the points weren't impressive enough to get him called back up to the NHL.

However, Armstrong did leave his mark on the game. The guy who has one hockey card is responsible for something that tons of kids, and old beer league wannabes like you and me, try every now and then. It's something that most of us only wish we could do: the lacrosse style goal. Bill Armstrong called it the "High Wrap."

You've seen the move. You're behind the net and you whip the puck on to your blade, raise your stick in the air and fire the puck into the top corner. Sidney Crosby made headlines when he did it in the Quebec Major Junior Hockey League with the Rimouski Oceanic. Mike Legg did it for Michigan in the 1996 NCAA tournament. Well, Armstrong was the first. In fact, he taught Legg the trick during the off-season back home in London. Unlike Legg and Crosby though, Armstrong didn't make any headlines when he was doing it. It all started innocently enough, with Armstrong goofing around during the summer at hockey schools. Soon enough he brought the move to the pros.

"At the end of practice, we'd always end up having games and other things to kind of take away the stress. You just start doing some things with the puck, and next thing you know it becomes second nature. For me it was second nature. I'd do it in an exhibition game, or we'd have East-West games or U.S.-Canada games in practice and we'd always do it against the other team."

After seeing it countless times in practice, Armstrong's teammates were impressed. "Do it in a game, do it in a game," they would say. Eventually he did.

Armstrong scored on the "High Wrap" with the AHL's Albany River Rats. Whenever he'd end up behind the opposing goal, the home crowd would yell, "Do it!" The goal garnered its fair share of local press, but you would think a goal like that would make national headlines. That a goal like that would show up on highlight shows from coast to coast. It didn't. Why not? The answer is kind of simple.

"I had done it, like four times before Mike Legg had done it. But when you play in the American League, at that time, they didn't have very good video of games. So my PR guy in Albany was sending the tapes in to ESPN and they were turning it down because it was too grainy and it wasn't good quality video."

Bad video was responsible for Armstrong not showing up on your TV in the mid-'90s. It didn't matter though: he kept making the move as he went from team to team. During the '95–96 season he was doing the high wrap with the IHL's Detroit Vipers. Sure enough, one day the high wrap became very much en vogue, courtesy of Michigan's Mike Legg.

"The ironic thing about the whole move that Mike Legg did was I was playing with the Vipers in Detroit at the time, and I did it on a Saturday night game in Cleveland against the Lumberjacks. They had it on good tape so they sent it in [to the TV stations], and the next day Mike Legg had that game where he did it on national television so it was broadcast all over the place."

That's proof that in sports and in life, timing is everything. Armstrong kept doing his high wrap as he made his way through the minors. "I did it twice in one week with the Orlando team." It was a move that always drew a ton of attention, but he never considered it to be hot-dogging.

"I never really looked at it as showing anybody up. It's a legitimate play. It counts in a game and if it's going to help my team win, why wouldn't I do it?"

Armstrong's pro career ended after the 1997–98 season. He had one heck of a move and one hockey card to show for it. The move still shows up in beer league hockey. "Oh yeah, all the time. Guys laugh at it, and they want to do it. It's like second nature and they've seen it so many times they don't get too excited anymore."

As for his hockey card, he used it for a while in a promotional campaign when he started his realty career. It didn't take. "I found that it didn't work too well. Just because most people are more concerned about a good realtor than they are somebody who's an ex–hockey player with an NHL card."

That card still shows up at his office though when fans look for his signature. Once in a while an Armstrong will show up on eBay as well. And just like in a locker room, Armstrong's teammates, now in the form of fellow real estate agents, let him have it.

"The big joke is my card was on eBay at some point for seven cents and they were joking around saying, 'You're not worth anything' or something and it was a big joke. I say to them, 'Well, at least I have one,' that kind of shuts them up."

He's right. He has one more card and one more slick move than most of us will ever have.

MARK LOFTHOUSE 1980–81 OPC #331

In the fall of 1980, Mark Lofthouse had 138 NHL games under his belt. At 6-foot-1 and 192 pounds, he had decent size, but he also had a fantastic hockey pedigree. The Caps took him with the 21st pick of the 1977 draft after he led the Memorial Cup champion New Westminster Bruins in scoring with 112 points. And in the fall of 1980, for the first time in his hockey career, Mark Lofthouse had his very own hockey card.

"It's always a threshold to reach. I was pretty excited about the fact that I was in the NHL and that just kind of substantiated it," says Lofthouse, now a real estate agent in the Vancouver area. "It wasn't a big moment for me as much as scoring my first NHL goal or playing my first NHL game or playing at Madison Square Garden or playing at the Forum in Montreal. Those things are more memorable. I think that was more kind of 'Oh. That's kind of cool, I'm on a hockey card.' And you just think there's going to be more to come, I guess."

But there were no more cards to come. Number 331 of the 1980–81 set is the only card documenting Mark Lofthouse's career. He played just three games with the Caps that season. He spent most of the year in Hershey where he led the AHL in scoring with 103 points. After that season he only played in 40 more NHL games, with Detroit. He spent the rest of his career in the minors.

"Unfortunately I played on the worst teams in the NHL at the time. Washington and Detroit were at the bottom every year. I always tell people, when they say, 'How come you guys were so bad?' I just tell them, 'They didn't play me enough.'"

As for his one hockey card, Lofthouse says he always gets the same question from people when they slap it in front of him. "A lot of people ask, 'What's going on? Like, is it the national anthem? You've got your hand by your heart . . . I mean, that's what it looks like.' 'No!' I hated my shoulder pads and they were always kind of coming forward on me and I know 100 percent I was readjusting my shoulder pads. And that's why I've got my hand up by my heart because I'm pushing my shoulder pads. It's kind of an oddity I guess from that picture. Kind of a unique moment."

Thanks to those shoulder pad problems, another thing stands out about the card: the No. 8. Back in the early '80s, Lofthouse was a sniper in the Caps organization. He did most of his scoring in the AHL though. These days, another No. 8 in Washington does his scoring at the NHL level.

"My claim to fame is I wore No. 8 with Washington, so that's the one I'm holding on to the most. I told [Alexander] Ovechkin, 'When they retire our number, I'd like to be there.'"

The No. 8 isn't Lofthouse's only claim to fame. Read his bio on the back of the card: "He's a tall and rangy winger who possesses a good shot and the knack for scoring goals in bunches." On December 9, 1978, Mark Lofthouse picked the perfect time to get hot. His Capitals were in his hometown of Vancouver. Lofthouse scored three goals in a 7–5 Washington win. But that's only half of the story. He got his hat trick on the same night he almost lost three fingers on his right hand.

Yes, this story might make you queasy.

"I was just taking my glove off on the bench. It was late in the first period. I took my glove off, put my hand down on the bench and then Guy Charron jumped up on the bench—you know, like you jump up off the bench and over the boards. So his skate landed right on my hand and he pushed off all his weight." Lofthouse's right had was sliced. Charron's skate dug deep into three of Mark's fingers. There was blood every-where. Luckily for Lofthouse, Charron's razor-sharp blades did not slice all the way through his fingers.

"I think the shock of it was more than the pain. You think that you're going to lose your fingers." The Caps trainer immediately rushed Lofthouse to the dressing room. Then the stitch work began. By the time Lofthouse was sewn up, the second period was about to begin. Lofthouse had a ton of friends and family in the stands, about 300 he figures. He never gave much thought to the idea of calling it a night.

"I didn't even know if I could hold on to my stick properly." It turns out he could. A potential nightmare turned into an absolute dream for

Mark Lofthouse. He put on a show for his 300 family and friends and the rest of the Pacific Coliseum. Pucks started going in the net—he scored one, then a second. Eight minutes and 18 seconds into the third period, Lofthouse beat Glen Hanlon for his first career hat trick. It was Washington's first ever win in a Canadian rink. "I wasn't going to let anything stand in my way and I went out and played. I got first star.

"It was a very surreal night for me. It was great to do it in front of family and friends. I still have people come up who were at that game and they remember that moment."

But then things went from really cool to cooling off for the then 21-year-old. Lofthouse went from scoring a hat trick to riding a bus with Hershey in a matter of days.

"Ryan Walter [who centered Lofthouse the night he scored the hat trick] tells the story every time I see him and we're around people. He says, 'Lofty was the only guy you ever saw score three goals and a week later they send him to the minors.' Which is pretty much what happened to me. That [hat trick] was a special moment obviously because I had so many people there. I thought it was kind of the beginning of a lot of big things. But I had a lot of good things, a lot of good moments in my career."

Mark Lofthouse won a Memorial Cup. He won a Calder Cup as well. He scored a lot of goals too. His 281 career AHL goals are good enough for the 28th highest total in American League History. And he did manage to get his face on one hockey card.

"It was nice to have. I would have liked to have seen a few more."

He has no regrets about his career. Right now, he is more focused on another player: his son Trent is an up-and-coming prospect in the Western Hockey League.

"I think he skates better than I did. He's just starting to establish that nose for the net. He's got great hands. He's got a great shot." If all goes according to plan, maybe Trent will crack an NHL roster one day and end up on a few more cards than his old man did.

"I hope so. I'd be thrilled."

CRAIG FISHER 1990–91 OPC #126

Craig Fisher never thought he'd play in the NHL. His older brother had a bad experience in the OHL, so Craig decided to play Junior B. He just went out and played. Soon enough, he was drafted by Philadelphia—it didn't really shock him; he just kept playing. Then he went to Miami of Ohio for a couple of years. The next thing he knew, he had a deal with the Flyers. And in the 1989–90 season he suited up for two games with Philly.

"I kind of was a slow burner. I was never a big minor hockey star. I was the second best player. My brother was a lot better than me growing up. I got drafted, third round, out of Junior B, the Metro League. So I wasn't one of those [guys] that really thought about the NHL. I just loved the game, went to college and got a chance to play."

That is one casual rise to the NHL. "No big whoop" seemed to be the theme of Craig Fisher's road to the NHL. The scope of what he'd accomplished didn't set in until one day during the summer of 1990 when reality came knocking on Craig Fisher's door.

"I was in the house in Whitby and my brother and I were just kind of hanging around and I get a knock on the door. There's a FedEx guy out there and he's got something for me to sign. I open it up and it's a hockey card and a cheque. To be honest, I had no idea that I was getting a hockey card. So just looking at it the first time, honestly, it really was one of the most memorable moments." It was validation. It was real. Craig Fisher went from Junior B to the NHL in three years.

"I collected hockey cards. So for me to get a cheque for, I don't remember what the [amount] was, but for me to hold my card and get a cheque, I'm saying to my brother, 'You know, I would have paid anything to have a hockey card, let alone they're paying me.' Just talking about it now puts a smile on my face."

Hockey is timing, and so is life in the hockey card world. Fisher was in the right place at the right time; his NHL debut coincided with a hockey card boom. He also got 1990–91 cards from Score and Upper Deck. He's quick to tell you the Upper Deck version had Jay Wells on the front, "For a while there, it was worth five bucks."

Fisher's timing with the Flyers wasn't as great. He played two more games in '90–91. A few years later he had two short stints in the NHL with Winnipeg and Florida. When his career came to an end, Fisher had played in 12 NHL games. He never registered a point. He never got another card either.

Fisher's numbers at the minor league level, however, were astronomical. In 1995–96 he scored 74 goals for the International League's Orlando Solar Bears. "At that time if you look back, the IHL was considered the second best league in the world. They were paying great salaries," says Fisher, who ended up with 130 points for Orlando in 1995–96, good enough for second in the IHL scoring race behind former NHL sniper Rob Brown. "To me I'm as proud of that, or prouder than playing in the NHL."

The next year, after four games for the Panthers, marked the end of his NHL career. "[Hockey executives] always said I was not a fast skater. I think I probably wasn't quite good enough. I could only be a superstar kind of player, a goal scorer player, but I wasn't good enough to be an NHL goal scorer type of player because those guys, the one percent guys that are there, they are unbelievable."

Fisher's playing days ended suddenly when he suffered a devastating concussion while playing with the AHL's Rochester Americans. He took a suicide pass and was crushed as he collided with two opponents. "All three of us were going as fast as we could. So I had a little one [concussion] on the first hit, a huge one on the second and then I hit my head two separate times on the ice. The doctor said it was basically four concussions within three seconds."

Fisher was hauled off the ice and into the Rochester dressing room. He was placed on a medical table. While he was being checked over, player–assistant coach Randy Cunneyworth, a 38-year-old veteran of 866 NHL games, arrived on the scene.

"Randy Cunneyworth is a man's man, a super nice guy. All of a sudden he looks down and he starts stroking my hair, he was 10 years older than me. I remember thinking, my only thought, my only memory of that night is him doing that and I remember thinking to myself, 'How bad must I look?' He knew looking at me that I was never going to play again."

Hockey was over. Normal, everyday life became difficult. The concussion would not go away. The pain would not go away. For a year, Fisher slept 20 hours a day, he could not stand the daylight. For the next eight or nine years, Fisher says he went "underground."

Eventually Craig Fisher came back to the game. He took a gig as an associate coach at the University of Ontario Institute of Technology in Oshawa, Ontario. Soon enough, reminders of the old days started showing up, courtesy of Canada Post.

"All of a sudden, as soon I was kind of out there I started getting these cards. When I got the first one, I couldn't believe it. I've gotten them from Europe, the United States, so the first year I probably got about 30, 40 at least. I mean my first thought was why would anybody want my autograph still? That was my first thought, I just laughed about it." For the record, Fisher says he only signs the back of the Wells card.

Fisher now spends his time coaching Junior A hockey in Whitby, Ontario. It's not the Bigs but it's full of kids who want to get there. Fisher made it to the NHL in what he likes to recall as a much more innocent time. These days, kids who aren't even good enough to make his team are rolling with an entourage.

"I coach Tier II. There's guys who aren't even able to play at my level who have agents and advisors. That's the way it's gone. Back in the '80s, it was not so corporate. I mean, the money wasn't so great. I mean it was great, but it wasn't like it is now. So you could go in and be a player and you could still be naïve to how things go."

Naïve enough to even be shocked that once you "casually" end up in the NHL that you may just end up with your very own hockey card as well.

"When I saw that hockey card, I wasn't a guy, the guys now, who've gone through the OHL, they've been kind of managed on interviews and they're ready to take that step. To me, even though I'd already played in the NHL, seeing that [card] was surreal. 'Surreal' is used a lot, but it really was. Because I was like, 'Who is this guy that I'm looking at? Is that *me*?' It was a special thing."

Frank Spring 1975–76 OPC #341

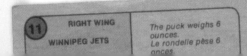

"They sucked." Frank Spring is talking about the uniforms worn by the California Golden Seals. "I just thank God [that] I missed the white skates. But now I shouldn't say thank God because I know a couple of players that have them. They're worth a fortune . . . I kind of wish I would have been there for that." The white skates were no more by the time Frank Spring joined the Seals in 1974–75. His 28-game appearance in the Bigs was enough time to land him his one and only hockey card.

"I remember the day they took [the picture]. We were playing against the Maple Leafs. And we were up there. And we went for our morning skate and that's where they took it. You pretty much do your own pose. They didn't really bother you much. You just bent over and held your stick and that was about it. They did it in the dressing room."

And with that quick pose, Frank Spring finally had a card. His hockey journey began in Cranbrook, British Columbia. His life as a pro began in 1969 when he went fourth overall to the Bruins. "When I was drafted, I found out on the ticker tape at the local radio station that I went first to Boston. So it's a little different now. They pay money now."

Spring's first deal with the Bruins was for $8,000, along with a $12,000 signing bonus for a grand total of 20 grand, not bad. It was goodbye Cranbrook and hello Bobby Orr and the Boston Garden. "The first NHL game that I ever saw I was playing in it. So that's pretty intimidating. That was in Montreal. That was the first exhibition game I played with Boston and my legs were shaking. I was 19 years old out of Cranbrook and had never seen an NHL game."

The stats on the back of Spring's card have a huge gap. They only show his NHL stats, one game in Boston, five in St. Louis and 28 with California. Part of his bio reads, "Short on big-league experience." But by the time Spring got his card, he was not short on pro experience. He had made minor league stops in Oklahoma City, Hershey, Richmond and Denver. The life of a pro hockey player may sound like a dream to those of us who have never been there, but Spring says life in the minors in the 1970s was tough—really tough.

"I think it was harder to play in the minor leagues than it was in the NHL. I believe that today. I came up with guys like Dave Schultz and the Broad Street Bullies. I played with all of them in the minors. And I played against them too. It was rough. There's guys up there trying to get up to the NHL and I realized years later it's easier playing up here [in the NHL] because the players are better and, as a whole, a little quicker and stronger. It was really strange but I found it that way."

And if you wanted to live the dream and make it to the NHL, you did anything, and played through anything, whether it was a broken nose or a concussion. One night in Cleveland, Spring's Richmond teammate Dave Schultz stick-checked an opponent. The opponent's stick caught Spring in the face. Smash—he had a broken beak. It didn't matter. He didn't miss a shift.

"I would go off the ice and the trainer would stuff gauze up my nose, both nostrils. I'd go back out. I could hardly breathe and play the next shift. And then come back to the bench and he'd take those out because they were full of blood and put new ones in. That's the way it was in those days. And I didn't want the players to think I was a sissy. And I look back now and I was concussed then too and I look back now and I say, 'Frank, what an idiot you were.'"

Another thing that the back of the card does not fill you in on was the toll life as a minor-leaguer took on Spring's family. "I was in Richmond, Virginia, which was Philly's number one farm team at that time and playing with Schultz and MacLeish and Saleski and all those guys. And I got traded to St. Louis and I was in San Diego. And my wife was still in Richmond and I had a little boy. I never saw him until he was a month old. So that's pretty rough on a family and pretty rough on a player, you know. But in those days I had to play."

Sometimes hockey doesn't make a lot of sense either. After leading the Central League with 44 goals in '75–76, Spring got another shot with the big club. By this time the Seals had made their way to Cleveland and were known as the Barons. Spring played in 26 games for the Barons. He scored an impressive 11 goals and added 10 assists for 21 points. "Today a guy that does that is making a lot of money."

But Spring didn't make a lot of money. Instead, he spent the next season in the AHL with a cameo in the WHA. He retired after that year, calling it quits after the '77–78 campaign. Spring traded in his stick and skates for life on the railroad. After a few years on the railways, he went into his father's auto sales business. He is still in auto sales. Two of his sons, including his son Corey, who played 16 games with the Tampa Bay Lightning in the late '90s, are also in auto sales.

Frank Spring is one honest guy, and it's a pleasure to speak with him. He looks at his pro career as a ton of fun, but also a ton of work. He went fourth overall in the draft, these days he'd be signing for hundreds of thousands of dollars. But he figures everything happens, and happened to him, for a reason.

"It's a good thing I didn't make any money because maybe I wouldn't be here now. I look at how immature I was and how backwards I was when I got there. If they would have given me a million dollars, I might be dead. I seriously think that that's part of the reason why I'm still here today. I really do. I don't think I could have handled it."

Sometimes a card only tells you part of the story. Especially when a player only has one card to show for nine years of pro hockey. "I had a lot of fun playing. But I wouldn't say it was the best thing. I had times there where I thought maybe I'd have been better to get a job and live at home, you know. Anyway I wouldn't give it up for anything either. Don't get me wrong. I saw a lot of places, had a lot of experiences and got to meet a lot of people."

And he got a hockey card out of it as well.

"I wish I would have had more."

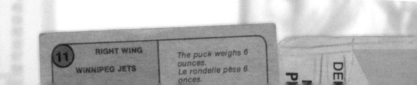

JACK VALIQUETTE 1980–81 OPC #108

Confession: I love the Colorado Rockies uniform. When I was a kid, the only times you'd get to see the Rockies were in magazines or on hockey cards. The Rockies never played on Saturday nights, or if they did, I definitely missed the games. And when you'd finally get to see Monday night's highlights on Tuesday's six o'clock news,

Chapter Eight

THE '80s

the Rockies never made the cut. Why would they? They weren't exactly a marquee draw. During their six seasons in Denver, they won a grand total of 103 games, which, on average, is a little over 17 wins a year. They didn't win on the ice, but in my eyes they were a hit. I loved pulling out the odd Rockies card from a wax pack. I loved the way they looked: the blue, red, gold and white just worked for me.

Which brings us to card number 108 from the 1980–81 O-Pee-Chee set. It's Jack Valiquette, and I'm sure you're asking the same question I am. What is covering his right ear? The old CCM helmet was classic. Basically all the cool kids wore one, but only Valiquette had some kind of magical large blue ear patch. Turns out it was not just for aesthetic purposes; the patch was very much needed.

"I had broken my cheek bone," Valiquette begins. "I had been hip-checked, if you can believe it. My head went right into the boards. I missed about three weeks and had a patch put over the side there."

Get ready for some gross injury detail.

"They had to pull the bone back out. I had a scar

there, but that's what happened there. Protection over that cheek, just at the side of my ear actually."

So now I have to ask a question—how do you hurt your cheekbone if you're the victim of a hip check? Get ready for some more gross injury details.

"Two of us were going to angle each other along the boards. I braced myself for the hit and the other guy and I went down. I think we were playing against Minnesota. So I went over too and another guy was coming in, I think it was Paul Shmyr, and he just hit me. But what happened was, I went head over this other guy and he hip-checked my head into the boards."

So Valiquette was hip-checked, but it wasn't hip on hip. It was hip on face. "That didn't feel so good. I got up and I went to take the faceoff. I took my glove off and I said, 'Man.' I could feel there was an indentation at the side of my face there." This all sounds very painful, but at this point, Valiquette, one of the game's great storytellers, simply laughs at the memory of his face being partially caved in. "I didn't think it was that serious but then I felt that. I said, 'Oh, there's something wrong here,'" he says to even more laughter.

So that is the story behind this very necessary fashion accessory for Valiquette. What you don't see on this card, and what perhaps was not in the picture at all, were Valiquette's skates.

For a time Valiquette tried to get all '80s New Wave when it came to his blades. Around 1980, a different kind of skate hit the market. I had a pair as a kid that were made by Orbit. Basically the skates were giant plastic boots. You put your foot in a slipper and slid it in the giant plastic boot. They were clunky, awkward looking and made up of what seemed, at least in my memory, to be an extremely large amount of plastic.

Valiquette saw the future of skate technology one summer while working at a hockey school. The future was Lang, as in giant plastic steel-bladed Lang hockey boots. I mean, skates. Valiquette was impressed with the new technology. His coach in Colorado, the legendary Don Cherry, was not.

"They were very comfortable. So I said, 'I can probably play the season in these.' Anyways Grapes, at training camp, he said, 'Those skates are no good. Get rid of them.' I said, 'No, no, they're okay. They're okay.' So I go through camp and start the season. If you cut really hard on them, sometimes [the slippers] actually slip out on you. So not being a gifted skater, anything that made it worse wasn't good, so about a month in [Don Cherry] told me, 'Get rid of those skates. They're no damn good.' I said, 'No, no.'"

The dance continued between Valiquette and Cherry until one night things came to a head. With Valiquette lumbering around the ice, his coach just couldn't take anymore. Cherry's words to his centre were blunt and to the point.

"'Get off the ice' he said. 'You look like a Clydesdale!'" It was tough to argue with that. Take a look at an old pair of Langs. Now take a look at a Clydesdale. Don Cherry was bang on. "So I got off the ice and I changed my skates. And the next month I was player of the month for Colorado. So it seemed to work out." There's a reason why Don Cherry was a Jack Adams award winner. "I got rid of the Langs and put on my Bauers again and away I went." Jack Valiquette scored 23 goals for the Rockies in '78–79 and then 25 in '79–80.

Valiquette only played 25 more NHL games after the '79–80 season. This was his final card, one with a pretty cool story thanks to a little blue patch.

BRIAN PROPP

86 HEIGHT: 5'10" WEIGHT: 190 SHOOTS: LEFT

Born: 2-15-59, Lanigan, Sask. Home: Regina, Sask.
Last Amateur Club: Brandon Wheat Kings (1978-79)
Acquired: 1st Round Choice (14th overall) 1979 Draft

NHL RECORD/FICHE DANS LA LNH

Year Année	Team Équipe	GP	G	A	PTS	PIM
79-80	Flyers	80	34	41	75	54
80-81	Flyers	79	26	40	66	110
81-82	Flyers	80	44	47	91	117
82-83	Flyers	80	40	42	82	72
83-84	Flyers	79	39	53	92	37
84-85	Flyers	76	43	53	96	43
85-86	Flyers	72	40	57	97	47
NHL Totals/Totaux dans la LNH		546	266	333	599	480

1985-86 Game Winning Goals: 5
Buts gagnants en 1985-86: 5

Brian scored his 500th NHL Point vs. NY Islanders, 4-4-85.
Brian produisit son 500e point dans la NHL, contre les Islanders, le 4 avril 1985.

© 1986 O-Pee-Chee
NHLPA
Pts. in Canada /Imprimé au Canada

NHL
NHLPA

BRIAN PROPP
LW ◆ FLYERS

BRIAN PROPP 1986–87 OPC #86

Who wouldn't want to be Brian Propp in the mid-1980s? The guy looked like a hockey player. He had the blond, wavy mullet to go along with that awesome Flyers uniform. He was on a rock solid team and he was a rock solid player.

Now flip the card over and look at Propp's numbers. One word comes to mind: solid. He racked off five straight 80-plus point seasons. Propp and his Flyers were styling, but first let's focus on his styling mid-1980s look on the front of the card.

"Looking back, we all change our dress code, our hair length and our type of hair and facial hair. Early on in my career, I used to get a couple perms and have curly hair through the perms and as I got a little bit older I just kind of had more of the business cut, and shorter hair."

Well, thank goodness this card is well before Propp decided to go all business and was still rocking the mid-'80s hockey look. Propp says it was just the style at the time. You had the flow and you had the look, even if you didn't think about it too much. "I just remember we were just very comfortable, confident, skating around. You had to have a little bit of an attitude and not worry about what you looked like."

Propp's Flyers were a confident bunch. They were a solid hockey team. The Flyers met the Edmonton Oilers on two occasions in the Stanley Cup Finals, in 1985 and 1987. The Oilers won both times. "We battled through the east to get to the finals and then going up against Edmonton, they kind of breezed through the other divisions and were pretty well rested and very healthy. We were very banged up both in '85 and '87 but we just played that team game and everybody was playing for each other and we were grinding it out and we almost pulled it off in '87."

The Flyers took the Oilers to seven games in the spring of 1987. The Oilers won the seventh and deciding game of the finals 3–1 on May 31st. It was a tough series. No love was lost. But just a couple of months later, four Philadelphia Flyers and five Edmonton Oilers would wear the same jersey when they suited up for Team Canada.

Brian Propp played in what is arguably one of the greatest hockey tournaments of all time, the 1987 Canada Cup. The best-of-three final between Canada and the USSR was wide-open, end-to-end hockey. For anyone of my generation, it inspired a "Where were you?" moment when Mario Lemieux scored with 1:26 to go to give Canada a 6–5 win in the third game.

"When you play that long in the '87 Finals, that was our 26th game, you were just so exhausted, win or lose, it's hard to know how close you were to winning the Cup. You are just so mentally and physically drained it takes a while for it to sink in a little later. But a couple months later being with Team Canada, playing with Wayne and Mario, and all the great players that were there, I mean that was just an honour."

Propp literally played with Wayne Gretzky and Mario Lemieux. He was on a line with 99 and 66, skating with two of the greatest players of all time. But the man who went on to score 425 goals and over 1,000 points in his NHL career was not intimidated. He looked around the room and knew that if Team Canada was going to win, he had a job to do.

"I looked at it as I'm not here to look at Wayne and Mario and just think that they're going to do it all. We had a job to do too. I think I was the oldest player on the team that year [he was, at 28], so . . . my mindset was don't just be satisfied by being here. You know you've got to participate and if you want to win, you've got to have that mental feeling and positive leadership.

"I did get a chance to play with Wayne and Mario throughout most of the tournament. Different games Mike [Keenan, Canada's head coach] would switch different players and put them with different people. So it was such a good leadership room that people understood how to adapt to whomever they were playing with. That it didn't really matter and that's why we did so well, because we had such great leaders and players who knew their roles and also knew how to adapt with different players."

The three-game final was heart wrenching. No lead was safe. This was a time when the neutral zone trap did not exist. Neither did the neutral zone, for that matter. We just used to call it centre ice. Every game ended in the same score of 6–5. In Game 3, Team Canada spotted the USSR a 3–0 lead in the first period. It was 4–2 USSR after one, 5–4 Canada after two. Canada won 6–5. It was heart pounding, all-out entertaining hockey. Team Canada was flying and so were the Russians.

Here's Propp on Keenan's game plan to shut down the USSR: "You try to keep them to the outside and you always had to watch, because they liked to skate up the middle and then drop it to somebody coming from behind. And today if you watch some power plays, a lot of power plays do the same thing. They skate up and then they have somebody coming full speed from behind. We learned a little bit from it 25 years ago.

"It was such a wonderful tournament and a three-game series. I don't know if they have three-game series anymore. When you look back at that, I mean people look at that three-game series sort of like the '72 Series where it kind of had everybody glued to their TV sets for that week.

"I think we played a little bit more physical against them in the second and third games, which kind of helped us a little bit."

After the '87 Canada Cup, Propp played in Philly for another two and a half seasons. He went on to make stops in Boston and Minnesota before he wrapped up his career with the Hartford Whalers in 1994–95.

His hockey career started when hockey cards were just for kids. When he retired, his cards were all over the place. Brian Propp had a ton of different cards thanks to the boom of the early '90s. In 1986–87, Propp had no problem collecting all his cards from that season. There were two, and they both had the same picture, a Topps version and an O-Pee-Chee version. Propp has this mulleted hockey card. He's done a great job over the years tracking down the rest of his cards as well.

"I've tried to collect all of my cards over the years because I've got 16 nephews and nieces and I try to get a full set for everybody." What's their reaction to the old pictures of Uncle Brian? "I think that they just kind of laugh."

"There were some different cards where the action shots were pretty neat. I know there was one when I was playing for the North Stars that I was kind of flying through the air. My wife and children really like that one."

And you have to think they have a soft spot for the mulleted Propp from 1987, who is just about to embark on a Stanley Cup Final, followed up by one of the greatest hockey tournaments of all time.

MERLIN MALINOWSKI 1983–84 OPC #142

If you grew up like me in the 1980s, you simply had to have them: Cooperalls. And there they are, in all their full-length glory, on Merlin Malinowski's final hockey card.

I didn't have a green pair of 'alls. Mine were black. And they remain, to this day, the greatest Christmas present I have ever received.

It was Christmas 1984 and the only thing I wanted were a pair of Cooperalls. All the cool kids had them. I was one of the few kids on my minor hockey team that had yet to embrace the new fad, but man did I want to. My parents heard about my desire to ditch the socks and go with the pants on a daily basis. I am sure I drove them quite mad.

When Christmas morning arrived, I could hardly contain myself. Once Dad completed his usual Christmas morning ritual of torturing us kids by waiting to get ready for the day, my brother Pete, sister Kate and I headed to the tree. I knew my Cooperalls would be there. Sadly, they were not.

I was bummed. I was a joyless Christmas soul ripping through my presents that morning. Nothing was pants shaped. All the cool toys were never wrapped and there were no signs of any suddenly fashionable hockey pants anywhere.

Soon enough everything had been torn open by my tiny hands. No Cooperalls. I was stunned, shocked, and from what I can recall, very angry. I didn't hold back my emotions. I let Mom and Dad and Santa have it.

That's when my old man's master plan neared its climax. "What's that under the back of the tree, Kenny?" I dove in. There they were. Cooperalls. I immediately put them on and kept them on for the rest of the day. My cousins wore dresses and fancy shirts at Christmas dinner that night. I proudly wore Cooperalls.

And so did Merlin Malinowski during his one season with the Hartford Whalers, in 1982–83. "At that time I was excited to try them. I knew junior hockey was using them at the time and when I saw them I thought, 'Geez.' I liked the look and it was new so I thought it would be great," says Malinowski.

Thought. That is the key word. Like a lot of ideas that suddenly became fashionable in the '80s—feathered hair, acid-washed jeans and short shorts come to mind—Cooperalls didn't stick around for long.

Only two teams went with the hockey pants look, the Flyers and the Whalers. And before you knew it, 'alls were out. "To be honest, after a while, I don't know, it was like the novelty wore off about it. And just the tradition, I guess. You become a traditionalist. And it just wasn't the right look after a while."

So that was basically it. Cooperalls became a victim of the fashion police. You try rolling into the Montreal Forum on a Saturday night, skating around, looking up at the rafters, at the retired numbers of Beliveau, Richard and Doug Harvey . . . while wearing hockey slacks! "I wasn't sorry to see them go but it was fun when it first started."

Another thing that came and went almost as quickly as it started was Merlin Malinowski's NHL career. Check out the black print on the front of this card. It's not your classic O-Pee-Chee transaction summary. It's not "Now with Montreal" or "Now with Edmonton." It's "Playing in Europe."

After the '82–83 season, Malinowski had a choice to make. He could join the Pittsburgh Penguins AHL team or head to Europe. He went overseas. At 24, his NHL career was over. All these years later, he still thinks about the three words on the front of this card: "Playing in Europe."

"In retrospect, I wish I maybe would have stayed and taken a run through Pittsburgh. That was before the Mario Lemieux days, but they were coming, in just the next few years. So who knows, I might have had a chance to get up there and play with Mario."

Who knows what would have happened had Malinowski tried his luck in Pittsburgh? Flip the card over and give it a read. Part of his bio reads, "Appropriately nicknamed 'Magic.'" Magic Merlin and the Magnificent Mario. It has a ring to it, but it was never meant to be.

"I enjoyed my time over there [in Europe]. I just wish I would have exhausted all opportunities to play in the NHL." Europe did give Malinowski one huge opportunity: the chance to play for Canada at the 1988 Calgary Olympics. It was a homecoming of sorts for Malinowski, who was born in western Canada. After years in Europe, he got the chance to strut his stuff in front of his family and friends in Calgary.

"That was the ultimate hockey tournament," says Malinowski, who had three goals and two assists in eight games at the '88 Olympics. "That was such an amazing time and the highlight of my career without a doubt. You can thank Dave King [Team Canada head coach] for that. He's the one who kind of opened the door for me."

And that was it for Malinowski. He called it a career after the '88 Olympics. He spends a lot of time coaching now. His '83–84 card shows up every now and then. His young players get a kick out of his dated equipment. "Some of them have a laugh about it. They think it just doesn't look right. It's unique."

Unique indeed, and short lived. Cooperalls didn't last long. Maybe they just didn't look right. Or maybe it was because once you slid on the ice in them, you almost never stopped! But in the '80s, kids faithfully wore them to practice. And at least one kid even wore them to Christmas dinner. Merlin Malinowski wore Cooperalls for 75 games in his only season in Hartford. And now, whenever he wants to glimpse into the past, he can take a look at his only Whalers card.

"It's a favourite. There's no question. The whole pants are there . . . it's a piece of history. The older I get the more cherished that picture becomes. No question." And the more cherished those old Cooperalls become as well.

BOBBY SMITH 1983–84 OPC #181

When I was a kid, no other NHL team could hold a candle to the Montreal Canadiens. They were my team. They were my world. The only team that could run neck-and-neck with the Habs were the Pictou Mariners, my hometown Junior C team that used to destroy the competition. I could write a whole other book on the Mariners, but as far as the NHL went, the Montreal Canadiens had my heart.

In the fall of 1983, the Habs pulled off one big trade. Guy Lafleur was just over a year away from being prematurely pushed into retirement. Two of the big offensive guns for the Habs were Mark Napier and Keith Acton. I knew Napier and Acton were legit because in '82–83, Acton had an "In Action" card and Napier was on the Habs "Team Leaders" card. In my mind this more than solidified their status as solid offensive stars. Well, before I knew it, Acton and Napier were gone. They were on their way to Minnesota for Bobby Smith.

"I requested that trade," recalls Smith, who after five years in Minnesota figured he wasn't playing as much as he deserved and thought some new surroundings would be a good thing. "I was kind of waiting by the phone and I remember Lou Nanne [the Minnesota North Stars general manager] saying, 'Listen, I got Keith Acton and Napier and I'm holding out for a third-round pick.' And I said, 'Come on, don't hold up my career for a third-round pick.' But anyways [Lou] got it and I was off."

The trade officially came down on October 28, 1983. With a trade happening that late in the fall, and hockey cards set to hit corner stores in mere weeks, if not days, O-Pee-Chee definitely didn't have time for one of their patented airbrush jobs. Instead, Bobby Smith got the "Now with" treatment. There it is, on the bottom corner, standing out nicely thanks to the advertisement-free boards of the day. "Now with Montreal."

Acton and Napier were gone. Smith was a Hab, and in the winter of '83–84, I had the physical evidence to prove it. I likely picked up this card at the Hector Arena canteen during a session of what we called "after school skating." Or maybe I picked it up on the heels of a Saturday morning practice. Or maybe on a Saturday night, during a Pictou

Mariners game. (Yes, I spent a ton of time at the rink. It helped that I lived across the street.)

When I picked it up for the first time I asked myself the same question I do now, 30-odd years later. Why is the woman behind Bobby Smith sitting during the national anthem?

Turns out I've been wrong for the past 30 or so years. When you develop a belief as a kid, it's a hard thing to shake. For most of my life, I've firmly believed that the woman behind Bobby Smith, with the classic '80s haircut, in the classic '80s glasses, was sitting down during the playing of the national anthem. Come on. Stand up. Bobby is looking at the flag. He has his hand on his chest. It is such a patriotic moment. Wrong. As in, 100 percent wrong. Unlike Steve Hanson in the classic film *Slap Shot*, Bobby Smith was not "listening to the $%^&$# song."

"I think it was more like looking up at the clock you know, and seeing how much time was left on the power play or something," says Smith, now the owner of the 2012–13 Memorial Cup champion Halifax Mooseheads. "I had my helmet on too."

Now that I think about it, of course the song isn't playing. If it were, why would a guy who I deemed manly enough to put his hand over his heart not take off his helmet during the song. Well played.

As for the info on the card, the stuff that really matters, Bobby Smith was, yes, now a Montreal Canadien. "I arrived in Montreal and we had a home game the next day. It was an optional skate and I was the only guy. There was only a couple of us on the ice and I remember skating around and seeing my reflection in the glass with C-H on my jersey and thinking, 'Wow, this is really cool.' Because having grown up in Ottawa, you know, it was always about Toronto and Montreal."

The kid from 90 minutes down the road was now a member of hockey's most historic franchise. Nothing against Minnesota, it is the state of hockey, but the Montreal Canadiens are the Montreal Canadiens.

"It was shocking for me. I had come from Minnesota and we had a good team. We were in the semifinals one year and we were in the finals the next. So it's not like we were a team that hadn't made the playoffs in 15 years. But when I got to Montreal it was just far more serious. I remember one time being in the dressing room and we were in a tight series with Quebec, Guy Carbonneau saying, 'We can't lose this, I gotta live here. Ludwig, you're going back to Wisconsin, and Ryan Walter you're going back to BC, and I gotta live here.'"

And Smith's Habs had a major problem. They hadn't won a Cup in a whopping *four* years. "You really felt like you were the black sheep of the family. You know you had the old-timers' alumni room and Henri Richard is coming out of there and Dickie Moore and these guys and they have pockets full of Stanley Cup rings."

Soon enough, Smith would have his own Cup ring. Soon, that is, in the eyes of most of the world. Not so soon in Montreal, though. In the spring of 1986, backed by the goaltending of a rookie named Patrick Roy, the Montreal Canadiens, who finished seventh overall in the regular season standings, went on an incredible run. On May 24, 1986, Bobby Smith and the Montreal Canadiens defeated the Calgary Flames 4–3 in Game 5 of the Stanley Cup Final to win the 23rd Cup in Habs' franchise history.

"To win in '86, it really made it fun," says Smith, who was fourth on the Habs with 18 points in 17 playoff games during the spring of '86. "Really, seven years between Cups? Talk to people in Toronto and they don't feel sorry for you, but it was, you know, there was a little bit of 'Well, it's about time.'"

Smith spent seven seasons with Montreal before he found his way back to Minnesota after the 1989–90 season. This '83–84 O-Pee-Chee marked the start of his incredible Canadiens adventure. "I've said many times, I wouldn't want to start or finish my career with the Montreal Canadiens. Certainly at that point, it would have been really hard to have been a number-one pick coming in with the Canadiens. And on the other hand, I wouldn't want to be 35 playing with the Canadiens. But for me to be there, you know, I had seven really good years there. I was the leading scorer, the second leading scorer. We had good teams. We were in the finals or the semifinals a lot. And that was a great time to be a member of the Canadiens."

And cardboard reminders of his time with the Habs, including his '83–84 O-Pee-Chee, are never too far away. "I remember that card when it came out. I remember seeing my first NHL hockey card and thinking, 'That is really cool.' I've got every card that was ever made of me. I've got them in a box here."

Including the one that shows him *not* listening to the song.

CURT BRACKENBURY 1981–82 OPC #109

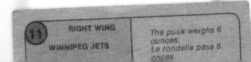

The wheels are in motion. Curt Brackenbury is in full flight. And chances are, for someone just out of frame on this '81–82 O-Pee-Chee, that spells trouble.

Curt Brackenbury was tough. And he came by his toughness and his work ethic honestly. After all, he says, one of the most influential coaches in his career was a man he encountered during his first year as a pro, the legendary hard-as-nails John Brophy. "Broph was absolutely critical in my development. As a matter of fact, I had it written in my contract that if I got sent to the minors I'd have to go where he is," says Brackenbury.

And Brackenbury ran into a few other characters along the way as well. That list of characters once included Jeff, Jack and Steve Carlson at the Minnesota Fighting Saints training camp. You might know Steve and Jeff better as two of the Hanson brothers from the movie *Slap Shot*.

"When they first came in that year to the training camp they had those glasses, they really parlayed that 'Stevie and Jeff and David Hanson' stuff into a wonderful sub career." The Carlsons went Hollywood. Brackenbury went north. In the fall of 1980, his career brought him to Edmonton. The Oilers had a stable of A-list talent in the making. Brackenbury was 28 years old, surrounded by some of the best young talent the game has ever seen. Gretzky, Messier and Anderson were all 19; Kurri, 20. And when Brackenbury looks at his '81–82 O-Pee-Chee, the memories come barrelling in just as fast as he used to barrel up the ice.

"It was so much fun just going to the rink. There weren't a lot of fancy systems. It was go out and get the puck and put it in their net as fast as possible. Then sprint back, line up and try to do it again."

Curt Brackenbury watched Wayne Gretzky rack up 164 points that year. He saw Mark Messier grind his way to a 63-point season in just his second NHL campaign. Jari Kurri racked up 32 goals. Glenn Anderson had 30. The young Oilers upset the mighty Montreal Canadiens in the playoffs. It was the beginning of something magical.

"I was there when they were learning . . . now this is my interpretation of it, but Slats [Glen Sather] was creating the understanding of how to compete. You've got to learn how to compete, you've got to learn what failure is and you've gotta try things and you've gotta fall flat." And it was what Brackenbury saw in practice that really opened his eyes to the amount of immense talent that the young Oilers had.

"After practice we would always go out and stay out and you played three-on-three . . . that little move that Glennie and Mess used to use, one would go behind the net and the other would come behind and they'd drop it back. A lot of that creativity and the development of the pattern came from those little games after practice."

And it was up to Brackenbury, the old guy at 28, to bring a little work ethic and a little wisdom to the young Oilers. "When you have a lot of nucleuses there, you need some glue that keeps the outside of the cell together. We had a lot of creativity and talent but we weren't playing in tune," says Brackenbury. "Creativity without discipline, it fills arenas, but it doesn't win in May and June . . . When the Oilers went out and became disciplined with their creativity, once they got the discipline, then they won four Stanley Cups."

Flip over Brackenbury's '81–82 O-Pee-Chee and read the stats. They'll tell you a bit about his role on that '80–81 Oilers team: 58 games played, 2 goals, 7 assists and 153 PIMS. There was another guy on that Oilers team who also racked up a few PIMS, who had a knack, just like Brackenbury did, for making "room" for his teammates. His name was Dave Semenko. "That was a lot of fun," says Brackenbury. "Semenko had a lot of skill . . . he could handle the puck and he could shoot, and yet a lot of people never saw that in his game. They only could see that he was that enforcer."

Brackenbury and Semenko were two tough guys who created their own little team within the team. "We had a little thing that we called the Swat Team. It was Swat One and Swat Two. We had a handshake and a headquarters and all these different things, all built around the basis of that's how you build chemistry within the team."

However, if you run into Semenko or Brackenbury, you won't be able to try that SWAT team handshake out. As any solid teammate would, even after all these years, Brackenbury is keeping the secret of the SWAT team shake in the locker room. He won't shake on the secret of the shake. "I don't think so, it's a personal handshake."

Brackenbury never raised a Cup with the Oilers. His playing days ended after the '82–83 season. But he didn't just hang around the cottage after retirement. This is a man who took part in an Ironman Triathlon in 1985. And if that wasn't enough, while he was lounging around Hawaii after the race, he was offered a chance to sail for a Canadian entry in the America's Cup. "I said, 'I've never been on a boat and I don't know what it is.'" Brackenbury jumped on-board anyway. And sure enough, things came naturally to him. On the boat, just like on the ice, he was a grinder.

"When you're a grinder, you do the same thing that you do on the ice except it was on water. We handled tough situations, we took care of things that needed to get taken care of and we were kind of the glue."

On his '81–82 O-Pee-Chee, Brackenbury was sailing on the ice. And he definitely encountered some supremely talented individuals along the way. When he looks at this card, he's reminded not only of what happened on the ice, but what happened off it as well. "Gretz was 19 years old then and he's signed by JOFA and then there's a bag right at your stall. He's signed by Mr. Big chocolate bars, there's t-shirts and 24 chocolate bars at every stall. He's signed by GWG, there's a jacket, shirt and pants at your stall. When I see [the card] those are the type of things I think about."

The question of who Brackenbury was about to sail into just moments after the picture on this card was taken, however, remains lost at sea.

PAUL MACLEAN 1982–83 OPC #386

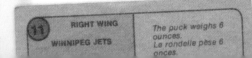

Just about every little town or village in Canada has some kind of connection to the NHL. You know what I'm talking about—this guy grew up here; that guy used to cottage here in the summer . . . But in Pictou, Nova Scotia in the mid-1980s we did not have much. In fact, we didn't have anything. Lowell MacDonald, who grew

Chapter Nine ERROR CARDS

up 20 minutes away in Thorburn, had retired from the NHL seven or eight years earlier. That's an eternity to a 10-year-old. Westville's Troy Gamble had yet to suit up for the Vancouver Canucks. And Pictou County's next generation of hockey heroes—Jon Sim, Colin White, Derrick Walser and Joey MacDonald—were younger than I was. They weren't going to make it to the NHL for a while.

The closest thing Pictou had to a "local" was Paul MacLean. He was from way down in Antigonish, a 45-minute drive away. I remember thinking, "Wow, an actual NHLer grew up just 45 minutes away from me!" I was amazed by that fact. I am still, kind of, today. So needless to say, if you were a kid from my neck of the woods, you had to get your hands on Paul MacLean's hockey cards. And if all worked out, you could get your hands on a Paul MacLean rookie.

I remember the first time I saw a MacLean rookie. I was about 12 at the time. His rookie card had come out a few years earlier, but this was the first time I remember seeing it. Like a lot of 12-year-old aspiring sportscasters

I considered myself somewhat of a hockey expert. I knew something was wrong right away. There was no way the guy on Paul Maclean's rookie card was actually Paul MacLean. Sure, the guy on the card had a moustache and feathered hair, just like MacLean did. But who didn't have a moustache and feathered hair in the 1980s?

I was bang on. It was not Maclean. It was "Larry Hopkins," says MacLean, the current head coach of the Ottawa Senators. MacLean doesn't know for sure how the fine folks at O-Pee-Chee got things wrong, but he does have a theory. A theory that, let's face it, is likely correct. "He had the moustache. I had the moustache. He had a way bigger head and a way bigger nose than I had. At the end of it anyway, there was not much either one of us could do about it."

But there was something that *Mrs.* Maclean could do about it. Paul's mom, back home in Antigonish, waiting for her son's first hockey card, was not impressed. "She wrote a letter to O-Pee-Chee expressing her disappointment in the rookie card not being the right one, and they sent her back an 8 x 10 with a nice letter of apology for the oversight." Of course Mom wasn't the only one back home who noticed that things weren't quite right on MacLean's rookie cardboard. His friends immediately noticed that an imposter had made it onto their buddy Paul's first ever hockey card. And they offered their condolences in the way only true friends could. "They all got a big laugh out of it, that they got the wrong guy."

Of course, after Mom's letter, O-Pee-Chee never made the same mistake again. Northern Nova Scotia's hockey hero went on to have many more hockey cards. All of them showed off MacLean and his trademark moustache. MacLean still has all his cards that were produced over the years.

"It's kind of [like] putting a stamp on an accomplishment. It's not like a great big award, but it's like an award. You can say that you have a hockey card. You know my brothers don't have one. My buddies don't have one. So it was kind of the start of a seal of approval, so to speak, that you made it to the National Hockey League and you're having an opportunity to play hockey for a living. And you should really appreciate the fact that you're good enough to have that opportunity. That's the way I looked at it."

So all these years later, is that card with Larry Hopkins on the front with Paul MacLean's name and stats on the back really a MacLean rookie card? All the hockey card checklists say it is. But what does the man himself think? "I think the rookie card is the first card. That's the first year I was in the league. It might have been an error but it has my name and my statistics on it," says MacLean, who scored a more than respectable 324 goals and 673 points in 719 NHL games.

"For me it was a bit of a disappointment but I figured there was going to be another one coming out, so it wasn't a big deal. And I figured somebody, some day, would write a book and talk to me about it."

Turns out the man whose hockey card career started with an error is right on . . .

TERRY CRISP 1975–76 OPC #337

There's something odd about Terry Crisp's 1975–76 O-Pee-Chee. He looks so . . . tall. And what happened to his trademark curls? I, for one, did not know that the man the hockey world calls "Crispy" was skilled enough to shoot both right and left handed. He's entering Gordie Howe territory now.

A lifelong left-handed shooter, Crisp is suddenly bearing down on the front of this card, ready to unleash the puck from the right side.

Surely something *isn't* right—because that isn't Crisp who graces the front of his '75–76 O-Pee-Chee. Instead it's the "Big Bird" Don Saleski.

It's easy to see why the error was made. Saleski was a 6-foot-2, 187-pound right winger. He shot right handed and had long flowing locks. Crisp was a 5-foot-10, 170-pound centre. He scored his 67 career NHL goals while shooting left handed. Anybody could get them mixed up. It's as easy as writing something sarcastic!

As soon as Crisp picks up the phone and the word *card* is mentioned, he begins to howl. He knows exactly what we're about to talk about. "Oh Saleski," says Crisp, "the one with Don Saleski's picture?"

Yep. *The Saleski.*

Crisp has no idea how the error occurred and no explanation for it either. He and Saleski are the furthest thing from twins. "No kidding, I'm good looking," howls the man who coached the Calgary Flames to their one and only Stanley Cup title in 1989. "Tell the Bird I said that." To this day, that old piece of cardboard still wreaks havoc. If you ever approach Crisp with the Saleski in hand—trust him—it's Saleski regardless of what you may think.

"I used to go to signings all the time," says Crisp. "Somebody would bring a card and they'd say, 'Mr. Crisp, would you sign my card?' I'd say, 'Sure.' They'd give me that one and I'd say, 'You do know that that's not me? That's Don Saleski.'" But fans can be a tough bunch to convince. After all, for years they'd been looking at this card thinking it had to be Crisp on the front. "They'd say, 'That's you!' I'd say 'Really, it's not me. I don't think you want me to sign.'"

Due to the confusion, Crisp was often left to feel the wrath of his fans. Or were they Saleski's fans? Crisp's name was on the card, so they had to be Crisp's fans, not Saleski's fans. But then again, it was Saleski's picture. So maybe they were Saleski fans. You can see how these interactions could get confusing. And sometimes a tad heated.

But eventually Crisp would give in. He would scribble his signature on his card that wasn't really even his. "They'd get mad at me," Crisp says of his fans, in dire need of his signature on the Saleski. So when Crisp signed it, he always gave a warning: "I'll sign your card, but I want you to know that that's Don Saleski, not me," says Crisp. "And they still wanted it signed!"

Crisp has a few Saleskis in his collection. He says he laughed the first time he saw it, and he hasn't stopped laughing yet. He only has one regret about the card. "At least they could have put my picture and Bobby Orr's stats or something . . . that would have been a whole lot better."

Well said, Crispy!

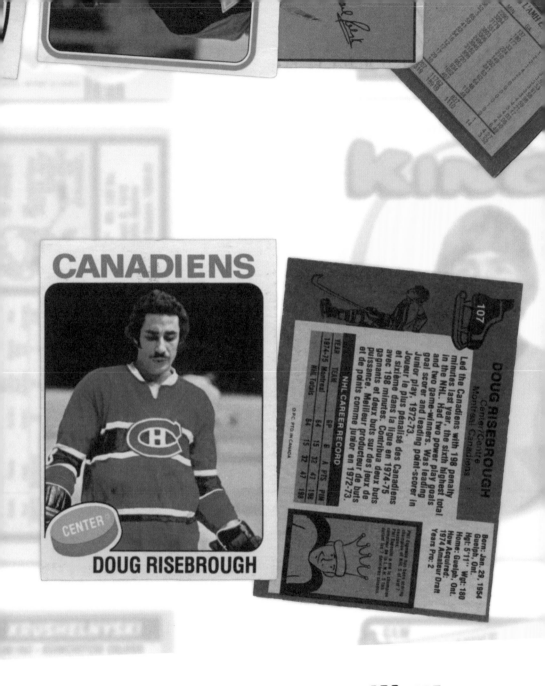

DOUG RISEBROUGH 1975–76 OPC #107

1980–81 OPC #275

Doug Risebrough is a lifetime hockey man. He's a veteran of 740 NHL regular season games, a winner of four Stanley Cups as a player on the 1970s powerhouse Montreal Canadiens, a winner of one more Cup as an assistant coach with the 1989 Calgary Flames—and he's a victim of a hockey card double whammy.

When somebody screws up on the ice, chances are someone else is going to benefit—when a defenseman coughs up a puck, someone is going to get a good scoring chance. Hockey card makers are no different. They make mistakes too. We all do. In Doug Risebrough's case, the hockey card makers made two mistakes. Risebrough was the victim of a case of mistaken identity on two of his hockey cards: his '75–76 rookie card and his '80–81 card.

Let's start with the rookie. One thing is for sure, that's not Doug Risebrough on the front of that card. Any fan can tell you, the man with the 'stache and the curly hair on Risebrough's rookie card is future Canadiens captain Bob Gainey. The mistake happened almost 40 years ago. But it turns out that Doug Risebrough has not been racking his brain for the last four decades trying to figure out how Bob Gainey ended up on the front of his rookie card.

"Somebody screwed up" is what he offers. When you think about it though, Gainey and Risebrough were ripe for confusing the card makers with their curly locks. Right? "Everybody had curly hair in the mid-'70s," says Risebrough, immediately shooting down your correspondent's theory.

The card mix-up doesn't seem to bother Risebrough all that much. He had bigger issues to tackle, like winning Stanley Cups. And that's what he, Gainey and the rest of the Montreal Canadiens did. The Habs won four straight Cups, in the springs of 1976, '77, '78 and '79.

Soon enough though, the hockey card makers struck again. When kids ripped open a pack of hockey cards in the winter of 1980–81 and took a look at Doug Risebrough, they were not taking a look at Doug

Risebrough at all. Once again, they were looking at a future Hall of Famer—this time it was Serge Savard.

Unlike the Gainey mix-up, Savard and Risebrough looked nothing alike. In this case, however, Risebrough has a theory of how Savard, a member of the Canadiens legendary "Big Three" on the blue line, came to grace the front of his 1980–81 hockey card.

"I never did hear the story but I suspected in that one, if you look at the picture of Savard, it shows he wore 18, and all you see is the 8. And so somehow maybe somebody saw the sweater and 8, and somebody that didn't have anything to do with hockey looked at the 8 roster on Montreal at that time and Doug Risebrough's name popped up." Now that's a solid theory. (A far better and more researched one than "Well, you and Gainey both had curly hair back in 1975 . . .")

On both occasions, it didn't take Risebrough long to figure out that he was the victim of mistaken identity, hockey card style. When you play for the Montreal Canadiens you are in the middle of hockey card madness. Fans are throwing your cards in front of you for autographs constantly. "They're coming to you and they're showing you the card with your name and you say, 'Well, that's not me.' And some people would say, 'Yeah, you're right,' and some people would tell you, 'This isn't you, but would you sign it anyway?'"

Risebrough doesn't see those old cards as much anymore. He's a scout now, but when he was coaching, the Gainey error and the Savard error always popped up.

And just like he did all those years ago, Risebrough still gets a kick out of the cards. Once a hockey man, always a hockey man. Risebrough offers up this final gem on the fact that two Hall of Famers are on the front of a couple of his hockey cards: "I actually took it as an insult when I saw both of those guys."

Steve Ludzik 1983–84 OPC #106

Larmer or Ludzik? Ludzik or Larmer? It's a question the card makers couldn't answer correctly in 1983–84. Steve Larmer ended up on Steve Ludzik's rookie card. Or did Steve Ludzik end up on Steve Larmer's rookie card? Both theories will do. I think.

Larmer-Ludzikgate is one of the most well-known mix-ups in hockey card history. It's easy to see how it happened. They have the same initials (more on that later), played Junior together, played in the AHL together and debuted with Chicago together. "Somebody lost a job there," says Steve Ludzik, one of the game's great characters.

Ludzik grew up collecting hockey cards. "It was the tastiest gum for about four or five bites and then it was just awful. I'd hate to have that stuff analyzed." He couldn't wait to get his hands on his own hockey card. Steve Ludzik is obsessed with hockey. You can read about his long climb up the hockey ranks in his excellent book, *Been There Done That*.

Once you've made the NHL you've made the NHL, but having your own hockey card? That's confirmation. Especially for a guy as obsessed with the game as Ludzik. And then it happened: Larmer is Ludzik. Ludzik is Larmer.

"I remember eagerly buying a couple of packs of O-Pee-Chee and opening it up. And you think your whole life about getting a hockey card. A real hockey card from the National Hockey League! You know, when I was a kid I loved hockey cards and collected them and did everything with them." Then it happened. Ludzik came upon his own card, or was it Larmer's? "I remember being shocked. It stunned me for a second. Larms and I were out in a mall or something like that when we got it, when we saw the card. And we were kind of going like, 'Jesus. That's kind of disappointing eh?' But when you think about it, it wasn't bad for me because I won rookie of the year!"

Always the optimist, that is a fantastic spin job by Ludzik, who coached in the NHL with the Tampa Bay Lightning and went on to a successful broadcasting career. What he says is true, Steve Larmer was the NHL Rookie of the Year in '82–83. It even says so right on the back of Larmer's card, "Steve was leading rookie scorer in 82–83 (43-47-90, 13 PPG) and won the Calder Trophy." There's only one problem though, Ludzik is on the front of that card. Hold on now, I'm confused. Isn't this part of the book supposed to be about card #106, the Ludzik card, not card #105, the Larmer card?

That brings us to a great question: which card does Steve Ludzik consider to be his rookie card? Is it the card with his face on it, or the card with his name on it?

"I would consider the rookie card the one with my picture on it, the one that says Larmer. It's just an eerie coincidence because we were so close for so long. Orville Tessier [their coach in New Brunswick and Chicago] called us the Bobbsey Twins."

So, is this story about Larmer or is it about Ludzik? Ludzik or Larmer? (They *are* easy to confuse.) In fact, they have even had their own problems with "Larmer or Ludzik"—or is it "Ludzik or Larmer"?

During their first year of professional hockey, Larmer and Ludzik roomed together in Moncton. They were playing in the AHL for the New Brunswick Hawks, two young guys with the world before them. And they were facing the challenges of bachelorhood, and there were numerous tasks to tackle, like cooking and laundry. Once a week Steve and Steve, Larmer and Ludzik, would head down to the laundromat, usually on a Thursday or Friday night. Now remember, these guys weren't multimillionaires, so they'd do their laundry together. As in, they'd throw it all in the same washing machine and dryer to save a few bucks. Problem? "We kept getting tired of mixing up our shit, eh? Our underwear, our socks and whose jeans are whose? So we said, 'We have to fix this up.' And Larms said, 'Absolutely right, we're going to initial all our stuff.'"

That definitely sounds like a plan that could work. However when you think about it for more than a tenth of a second, an obvious problem arises. SL is SL no matter how you cut it. You can label the undies "SL" but is that SL for Steve Larmer or Steve Ludzik? Perhaps it was a sign of things to come from O-Pee-Chee?

"We must have been tired that day because we initialled all our stuff and then we put it in the water and that and we were like, 'Oh, shit.' And Larms is like 'Larmer, Steve Larmer. Steve Ludzik? Stupid or what?'" says Ludzik. They had their lightbulb moment, but it was too late.

Then just a couple of years later O-Pee-Chee made the mix-up. It was never corrected. There are no corrected versions of their cards floating around anywhere. Ludzik's rookie card is Larmer's. Larmer's rookie card is Ludzik's.

"It was novelty. I just got back from Calgary last night from a speaking engagement. And part of my photo display was the fact that I had a mix-up card. And it's kind of deflating when you think about it because you want your own card. But you know what? Looking back now, 30 years later or whatever, it's actually something special, because if you're going to be mixed up with a guy, Steve Larmer ain't a bad guy to be mixed up with."

Unless, that is, you're trying to save a little money on your laundry.

STEVE LARMER 1983–84 OPC #105

We've heard Steve Ludzik's take on the Larmer-Ludzik epic hockey card mix-up. Now it's Steve Larmer's turn. "It's pretty self-explanatory" is the first thing Larmer says, trying to control his laughter.

These two were linked starting with their junior days in Niagara Falls. The hockey card mix-up only made the link stronger. And everlasting. Larmer and Ludzik have been stuck with it for the last 30 years. They'll be stuck with it forever.

"I didn't realize I was so ugly." Larmer's laughing again, recalling what went through his mind the first time he saw the card. "I said, 'Ludzy, I'm a lot better looking than this, right?' They made a mistake. What are you going to do, right? That's what will make it more popular than if it was done correctly.

"I think the stats were done properly. The only thing they got wrong on it was the name on the front of the card. They got the first name right. So they could just black out the last name and then it was all fine."

Wait! But the picture still wouldn't have gone with the stats! This is so confusing. Larmer or Ludzik, Ludzik or Larmer? We're almost back to square one.

If they somehow managed to straighten things out, to correct the Larmer-Ludzik, chances are Larmer wouldn't be howling about his rookie card three decades later.

And three decades ago Larmer and Ludzik were joined at the hip. Yes, once upon a time they did initial their laundry "SL" in an effort to tell their clothes apart while playing with the AHL's New Brunswick Hawks. "It's amazing I survived and lived," says Larmer of their time as roommates in Moncton. "We ate good. I did all of the cooking. Ludzy tried to cook some of his mother's breaded pork chops one night, and it was like a pork chop in between two scrambled eggs. So that was the last of his cooking. The grease was unbelievable."

But maybe the grease did some good. The duo had a great year in the AHL. Ludzik put up 62 points, Larmer put up 82. The next season they found themselves in Chicago. That's when Steve Larmer earned himself an opportunity that any rookie would salivate over. He was told he was going to play on a line with the magical Denis Savard.

"It was exciting but it was probably the most frightening thing in the world too, at the same time." Frightening, because he had to produce. When you play with Denis Savard, you are going to get your chances. You better finish them. "The best way I can describe Denis Savard in that era is, I mean there was Wayne Gretzky and Dale Hawerchuk and Mark Messier and I mean there were some great players back then. The Trottiers and all of that, but Denis was the one guy that every time he touched the puck people in the stands would stand up. It was *What are we going to see next?* He was just so quick and so creative and a fantastic passer.

"He was just unpredictable. There was nothing set about him and I think that's why he was so hard to contain because he didn't have the same habits every time he came down the ice."

Larmer cashed in on his linemate's creativity. The evidence is right there on the back of his rookie card. Or is it Ludzik's rookie card? Anyway it's the one with Larmer's name on it, but Ludzik's picture. The numbers: 43 goals, 47 assists and 90 points. "Steve was Chicago's #2 scorer in 1982–83."

The next fall, the card, or rather the cards, hit wax packs. Larmer was Ludzik and Ludzik was Larmer. So which one does Steve Larmer, who went on to score 441 goals and 1,012 NHL points, consider to be his rookie card? The answer is both. "We got two. We got two of each, that makes us special." Then Larmer gets a little serious when he's asked if there's anyone else he'd rather have been mistaken for on his rookie card. "Well, anybody that's better looking than that. No, I think when you look at it from that standpoint, I don't think it could have worked out any better. It couldn't have been any more ironic.

"We were best friends. It's not like we were two completely different strangers on different teams or anything like that either. It's kind of strange that way too."

No matter how you cut it, Larmer or Ludzik is the stuff of hockey card legend.

BRAD MARSH 1980–81 OPC #338

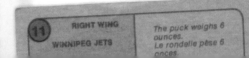

For Brad Marsh, card number 338 in O-Pee-Chee's 1980–81 set was confirmation that he had finally made it. Brad Marsh was a bona fide NHLer. Unlike today, when it seems like everyone has a card by the time they hit their mid-teens, Marsh had to really earn his cardboard. He had 160 NHL games under his belt before he

Chapter Ten   ROOKIES

finally made it on to a hockey card.

"Back in those days they didn't have the multiple cards that they do now for the juniors and so on and so on . . . I know you make it to the NHL and you have a nice contract but you didn't really appreciate making it until you got your own hockey card."

Marsh made it, but he was on the move. His Atlanta Flames were packing up and moving to Calgary for the 1980–81 season. Thanks to the move, Marsh's rookie card almost has a "What team do I play for again?" look. Yes, he's in Flames red, but where's the crest? It's not there at all. With the Flames on the move, the card makers simply airbrushed out the flaming "A" of the Atlanta club. It's an NHL card, but Brad Marsh kind of looks like he's playing for a men's league team that hasn't decided on a name or logo, rather than in the National Hockey League. "It was what it was, and some of the other guys were in the same position. So we all had a little chuckle over it, but it wasn't long after that that I got another card that came out with the Calgary 'C' on it."

The bottom line is Marsh was just pleased that he had a card. He's the first to admit, a lot of kids didn't go ripping through packs in the hopes that they would stumble upon some Atlanta Flames cards. The Flames didn't pop up on your TV on a Saturday night. So Marsh was simply thrilled just to be a part of the '80–81 set, not that he was exactly freaking out as he waited to make his cardboard debut.

"I never lost any sleep over it . . . being an Atlanta team, it's not like we were a hot commodity in the trading card business," says Marsh, who went on to become a hockey card regular throughout the years. "There weren't a lot of the Flames that had a card, let alone the rookie. It was kind of neat when it came out."

Along with the rest of his teammates, in the summer of 1980, the 22-year-old Brad Marsh and his logo-less jersey were on the move across the continent from Atlanta to Calgary. In Atlanta, the Flames were averaging just over 10,000 fans per game. The writing was on the wall; the team could not survive, so they packed up and headed out of town. "We had great fans in Atlanta, but there was just no corporate base there. And granted, there were no private suites back in the arena then, like there are now. They just couldn't make it work, but like I said, the fans were awesome."

Hockey wasn't a tough sell in Calgary, but Marsh had to endure three seasons in the "cozy" confines of the old Corral. Soon enough though, the Flames moved into the Saddledome. They've been there ever since. Marsh, in fact, sees some fans who think the Flames have been in Calgary forever. His old hockey card often makes a younger generation of fans ask a question: "Where's the logo on your rookie card?"

"A lot of people ask why it was airbrushed and you explain that we were in Atlanta and sold to Calgary. You know the younger generation of hockey fan; they don't really realize that the Calgary Flames are in some ways a newer team. They just weren't always there."

Like every old-time hockey player on the planet, Marsh has changed a lot since his rookie card came out. More than 30 years have passed since that "A" was airbrushed out, and that fantastic mop of hair is no more. However, his rookie card can still inspire, especially if the time is right. When a reporter, say, emails Marsh a picture of his old rookie card and asks to talk about it, the card can be a useful piece of evidence. It can reflect back to a time, and a head of hair, that once was.

"It's funny, we were at a disco themed party on Saturday and so I actually wore a suit. It was my Team Canada suit jacket from 1976, when I was at the World Juniors, and somebody gave me one of those black curly haired wigs. I just happened to have my phone with [a picture of] the card that you sent me and I called it up and I was showing everybody the hockey card with the full head of hair. And the wig that I had on was almost identical to my hockey card picture, like I said, and everyone had a lot of laughs over the head of hair that I had when I was 22 years old."

DEREK SMITH 1979–80 OPC #89

"That's the same year as Gretzky's rookie year, isn't it?" says former Buffalo Sabre and Detroit Red Wing Derek Smith. Yes, it is.

We're talking about Smith's rookie card. It came out in the same set as one of the most popular hockey cards of all time, the Wayne Gretzky rookie, but the two rookie cards have never been mistaken for one another.

"I don't think that was a concern. Wayne was pretty good."

For a lot of card geeks, myself included, the '79–80 set is one of the best ever made, and not just because of the Gretzky rookie. The set also features the last cards of Gordie Howe and Bobby Hull. But there is more to it that just that. I love the design. And who doesn't dig the cartoons on the back. Perhaps most of all though, I remember the blue borders from when I was a kid. As far as I can recall, the '79–80 cards were probably the first to ever tumble into my hands.

For Derek Smith though, he never really ripped through wax packs when he was growing up. Get ready to salivate hockey card nerds: Smith got all the cards he wanted, uncut, compliments of his dad. "A neat story about the O-Pee-Chee and the Topps cards—my father's company actually printed those. He worked for a company called Lawson Jones in London, Ontario, and they printed labels but they also did all, for years, the O-Pee-Chee cards. They printed them and sent them to O-Pee-Chee to put the gum in them. So what he used to do is bring home the uncut print sheets, which are really valuable now."

If that isn't enough to get you all geeked up, here comes the kicker. As we noted, Smith's rookie and the Gretzky rookie were in the same set. So guess what Derek's dad brought home from the factory to mark the occasion? Uncut sheets from 1979–80. "My '79 card was on the same uncut press sheet as Gretzky's rookie card. At one time I had five sets of those and I gave them away to the kids and they used to cut them up and put them on the spokes on your bike and now they're worth like six, seven, ten thousand dollars a piece."

Or more? Likely a lot more. It hurts just hearing that. Smith had a few cards over the years, and every year he made it onto an uncut sheet of cards his dad would bring a sheet or two back home. All but one of those sheets is still hanging around.

"The only issue I have is the uncut press sheet that I have that I'm on with Gretzky. It dry rotted and a tear went right through his card, right through the Gretzky card." Ouch, that still hurts, but at least he still has one of the sheets.

Flip the card over and look at the back of the Smith rookie. One of the great things about this set was the cartoons in the upper right corner on the back of the cards. This is the main reason I wanted to get hold of Smith. The uncut sheet story was a pure bonus. Smith's cartoon has to be one of the best in the set. A suave looking young player skates by a couple of lovely young ladies. Their hearts are literally right out of their chests. The caption reads, "Derek is one of the Sabres' most eligible bachelors." It looks cool. It sounds awesome. Truth be told though, the Sabres didn't have a very deep pool when it came to eligible young men.

"I get the business from that line all the time from people. That year there were only three guys on the team that were single. That was Danny Gare, Terry Martin and myself, so it wasn't like there was a whole bunch of us." Still though, if you break it down, the cartoon is accurate. Smith *was* "one of the Sabres' most eligible bachelors." One of three. "Danny usually got first pick . . . there wasn't much competition. But I've been married almost 34 years now, so it's a long time ago."

Smith's playing days are also a long ways behind him as well. He retired after spending the 1983–84 season with the Adirondack Red Wings, Detroit's AHL affiliate. He ended up playing in 335 NHL regular season games, scoring 78 goals and adding 116 assists for 194 points. And buried in his closet in his home outside of Buffalo is the perfect reminder of his rookie season, an uncut sheet from 1979–80.

"If I can fix that one up, I might frame that one set, the one sheet where I'm on with Gretzky."

MAPLE LEAFS

O-Pee-Chee

TORONTO MAPLE LEAFS

TITAN TPM1020

DAVID REID • LW

290 LW/AG · Toronto Maple Leafs
DAVID REID

HEIGHT: 6'0" WEIGHT: 210 SHOOTS: LEFT
LAST AMATEUR CLUB: PETERBOROUGH PETES (1981-82)
ACQUIRED: SIGNED AS FREE AGENT, 8-9-88
BORN: 5-15-64, TORONTO, ONT. HOME: OSHAWA, ONT.

NHL RECORD / FICHE DANS LA LNH

Year Année	Team Equipe	GP	G	A	PTS	PIM
83-84	Bruins				1	2
84-85	Bruins	8	1	0	1	2
85-86	Bruins	35	14	13	27	27
86-87	Bruins	37	10	10	20	10
87-88	Bruins	12	3	3	6	0
88-89	Maple Leafs	77	9	21	30	22
89-90	Maple Leafs	70	9	19	28	9
NHL Totals/Totaux dans la LNH		242	46	66	112	70

GAME WINNING GOALS/BUTS GAGNANTS 1989-90: 1

David hopes to fill a checking role with Leafs in 1990. • David espère améliorer la mise en échec des Leafs en 1990.

NHL PLAYOFF RECORD FICHE DURANT LES ÉLIMINATOIRES		GP	G	A	PTS	PIM
	1990	3	0	0	0	0
	CAREER/CARRIÈRE	10	1	0	1	0

NATIONAL HOCKEY LEAGUE LIGUE NATIONALE DE HOCKEY
OFFICIAL LICENSED PRODUCT PRODUIT LICENCIE OFFICIEL
©1990 NHLPA
©1990 O-PEE-CHEE CO. LTD.
TM NHLPA
PTD. IN CANADA IMPRIMÉ AU CANADA
PEE CHEE

DAVID REID 1990–91 OPC #290

I'm sure it is safe to say that just about every kid who ever ripped open a pack of hockey cards also dreamed about having their very own card one day and playing in the National Hockey League.

For most elite players, once they reach a certain age, they stop ripping open packs of cards and focus more on their quest to reach the world's best hockey league. Dave Reid was not like most players. As he rose through the ranks, he kept on doing two things: striving to improve his game and collecting hockey cards.

"Playing junior hockey, and as I got closer to my pro career, I realized, 'Hey, I'm going to be a professional hockey player.' That's when it became 'Hey, I'm waiting to get my hockey card.' As a kid when you got a hockey card, you were in the NHL."

The Boston Bruins took Reid from the OHL's Peterborough Petes with the 60th pick in the 1982 NHL entry draft. The wait for hockey card number one was underway. Reid played eight games for the Bruins in 1983–84. He did not get a hockey card.

For the next few seasons, Dave Reid went up and down between the Bruins and the American Hockey League. Though he desperately wanted a card, he knew the hockey card game. To be on one of your own in the 1980s, you had to be one of the mainstays on a team, or at the very least be in the right place at the right time.

"The pictures always seemed to come out of New Jersey or Washington. And I'd never played in those rinks early that I can recall. So I'm like, you gotta play in those rinks to get on the card."

Reid's first tenure with the Bruins came to an end after the 1987–88 season. He had 95 NHL regular season games under his belt but he still didn't have a hockey card. That wouldn't be a big deal to most NHLers, but Reid was a hockey card freak. Dave Reid, professional hockey player, NHLer, AHLer, couldn't get enough cardboard. "My first couple years pro, I'd come home and I still lived with my folks before I was married and I'd put an ad in the local paper, in the Etobicoke *Guardian*, to see if anyone was looking to sell or purchase hockey cards."

Sure enough, sellers were out there. Reid was doing his card buying in the days before the monthly *Beckett Price Guide* came out. This was well before the boom. Dave Reid, professional hockey player, would haul around an old price guide and buy cards by the ton, often from kids with their parents keeping a close eye on the transaction. Reid says he was always fair. He'd offer 50 percent of the book price for stars and buy commons in bulk. "You could walk in with 50 bucks and walk out with thousands of cards."

Reid's hockey card spending sprees were not limited to the summer months. When he was on the road in the AHL, he always knew where to go. Not for a few drinks with the boys, but where to go to find a few packs of cards. Of course, being a hockey card collector while at the same time being a hockey player came with a stigma. "Everybody thinks you're a geek when you're playing pro while riding buses in the American League . . . There was a place in Springfield called the Sports Collectors Closet. It may still be there. I have no idea. But it was just around the corner from the hotel. I'd go in there and I'd buy the boxes of cards and on the way back to Hershey we'd open them, [with] the guys at the back of the bus."

You can just picture it, a pro hockey team heading down the highway, all geeked up on hockey cards. "I'm there with guys like Tim Young [628 NHL games played] and Donny Nachbaur [223 NHL games played]—all these guys who are looking at you, 'What are you doing?' At that time I'd be buying the mid-'70s stuff in the boxes. I started in '84 so I was buying '77 and '78s, just before the Gretzky rookie set. We had a whole pile of Topps stuff [in the bus], so we'd be opening them on the bus and the guys would be saying, 'Oh man, this is great, this is great.'"

What a scene. The mid-'80s, the Hershey Bears bus cruising down the highway, full of laughter as they sift through some old hockey cards. All would be well, until Reid would tell his teammates that he was just a little more into the hockey card thing than they were. "As soon as you start [with] 'Yeah, I collect hockey cards,' they said, 'Ah, come on!' Everybody thinks you're a kid. But it was fun."

In the summer of 1988, Dave Reid signed with his hometown Maple Leafs. It was an ideal situation. He and his wife would live with her parents in Pickering. Training camp was in Newmarket. Reid made the drive most days, some nights he would stay overnight. He was a budding Leaf; surely as a full time member of the Toronto Maple Leafs Reid would get a card. Of course, having spent most of the previous season in the AHL, he still had to make the team. Camp was of vital importance. It was also a great chance for Reid to hoard more cards. Reid soon discovered that a small card store was located on his drive from his place to Leafs camp in Newmarket.

"I'd stop in there and I would buy a couple of [wax] boxes of the '85–86 set, which was [Mario Lemieux's rookie]. I'd buy them on the way up and sometimes we'd stay overnight for camp. I'd sit in after practice and I would sit and I would sort cards. I'd open every card. You know stupid me, I opened every box at the time. And so finally I went in there one day, and for the week I had stopped in there two or three times. The guy didn't recognize who I was. I hadn't played yet for the Leafs at the time and I'd been in the minors. And the guy says, 'Why are you buying all these boxes of cards?' And I said, 'I'll buy whatever you've got. I just collect and I just want to make sets.' And he says, 'Well, I'm not going to put any more out because you're buying them all.'"

At his first Leafs training camp, Dave Reid had been cut. Not by the Leafs, but by a card store owner. It didn't really matter though. Reid had more than enough cards to keep him entertained if he had to spend a night in Newmarket. "The guys would all go golfing after camp. But I wasn't a golfer. So I'd hang out and go back and open cards and sort cards." If you're wondering, Reid ended up with a ton of Lemieux rookies. "I ended up with a pile of them . . . I've got a couple left. I've got a couple signed for the kids."

Reid's first ever Maple Leafs training camp worked out as far as hockey cards went, and as far as hockey went as well. Dave Reid cracked the Leafs roster in the fall of 1988. He played in 77 games in '88–89. Just one problem: he was dissed by the card makers once again. Dave Reid, hockey player, hockey card freak, was not included in O-Pee-Chee's 1989–90 set.

"In the O-Pee-Chee set, they didn't have everybody and they had more teams coming into the league so it got to the point where I was hoping to get one. Hoping you had a good enough year to get one."

The next year Dave Reid did not have a better season in Toronto, at least as far as the numbers were concerned. He played in seven fewer games (70) and ended up with 28 points compared to the 30 he racked up the previous season. It didn't matter. Hope won out and Reid was about to hit pay dirt. Hockey cards experienced a rise in popularity in 1990–91. Upper Deck joined the fold along with Score and Pro Set. Cards were everywhere. For a purist like Dave Reid though, he had to be on an O-Pee-Chee card. Card number 290 in O-Pee-Chee's 1990–91 set was a long time coming for Dave Reid the player and Dave Reid the collector.

"It took a while," Reid says. These days Reid doesn't have to look far to see his rookie card. "It's still pretty cool. My rookie card sits in my office, the O-Pee-Chee one right now. Right alongside the '72 Stanley Cup from the '72–73 series. Those are the only cards I've got in my office."

As a full time NHLer and a hockey card freak, with the card industry booming, Reid and his Leafs teammate Alan Bester did a very logical thing. The two NHLers opened a sports card store. "It was nuts. We had a lot of fun with it. My wife worked in it and it was kind of around the corner from my house. It was great because it was such a big thing at the time with all the new cards and it was such a huge hobby. Everybody was collecting."

The store averaged about $1,000 a day in sales. Reid kept buying and selling, arming his store with the latest packs and some vintage pieces from his collection as well. Back in the day, if you came to finish off a set, the guy behind the counter could very well have had the same name and face as the guy on the card that you were looking for.

"I remember sitting behind the register and you're ringing someone in at the cash after they're purchasing. That was when people would come in and go, 'I need 20 cards for my set' and you'd go through your commons and you pull it out and you'd ring people in. I'd be behind the counter. I remember one guy said, 'Hey, you know if you ever see Dave Reid, tell him he's a pretty good player. He works hard and he's got a nice store.' I said, 'Thanks a lot, I'm Dave Reid.' The guy was shocked that I was behind the counter."

Reid was picking up cards everywhere. When he hit the road with the Leafs, he knew where the card stores were located in just about every NHL city. These days autograph seekers sit around hotels waiting for the chance to score autographs from NHLers. Back in his day, Dave Reid used to sit around NHL hotels looking to score hockey cards.

"I can remember going into Winnipeg and sitting in the lobby in the Winnipeg hotel and a guy coming in and he sold me the '64–65 Topps set—the tall boys. He came in and I bought it for about 750 bucks and I can remember coming home and my wife was just livid. At the time, I think I was probably making about 130k. That was a lot of money in 1990, but it's still not enough where you can go and take 700, 800 bucks and buy a set of cards. I got home and my wife was livid that I bought this set of cards from this guy. I thought, 'Oh well, that's what I do.'"

As we all know, those wild boom days are now over. Reid's store closed down shortly after he joined the Boston Bruins in 1991–92. He says it just wasn't feasible. Dave Reid still has thousands of cards. Like a lot of us hockey card nerds, he's not quite sure why he does it.

"I just enjoyed seeing the perfect stacks of cards all piled up. And the smell of the gum was addictive. You could open the packs and you could just stick your head in the box of the fresh cards that you had opened. To me I had to buy cards. I had to get cards. And if I had the set, no big deal, I wanted another set."

Every once in a while, Reid will still look through his old cards too. Whether it is spotting a superstar or unearthing an old seldom seen common, there's a little beauty in the history, and of course the hair. "Some of the hairdos on those guys were unbelievable."

Luckily for Reid, he was very well coiffed on his rookie card. Looking at it, it is a very simple card. Nothing really stands out at first glance. Dig into the story behind it though, and you'll discover that perhaps no one in NHL history wanted a rookie card more than Dave Reid. Some players had to wait longer for their first hockey card, but Dave Reid sure had to wait long enough.

MIKE McPHEE 1985–86 OPC #225

Mike McPhee never thought of making it as a pro hockey player. When he was playing for Port Hawkesbury in the old Nova Scotia Northumberland Junior B Hockey League, all he was thinking about was school. "I played one full season in Port Hawkesbury. I used to be a goal scorer down there. I had 50 goals in 30 games."

McPhee then took his sweet scoring hands to Rensselaer Polytechnic Institute in Troy, New York, where he studied engineering, and math was on the mind. Pretty soon though, one number took over all the others in his life. That number was 124. The Montreal Canadiens took McPhee 124th overall in the 1980 draft. All of a sudden, pro hockey, and not his school books, was on the top of McPhee's mind. By the '83–84 season, McPhee was skating in the Forum with the Montreal Canadiens. Soon, he had his very first hockey card. "It's actually pretty exciting. It's one of the things you remember. You remember winning the Cup. You remember the Stanley Cup parade. You remember your first rookie card. So I was pretty excited to see it come out," McPhee says.

Confession: for me this card was a big deal. As you know, I grew up a Montreal Canadiens freak. For a while I had this card tacked on my bedroom wall. The fact that I could watch a guy from little old Nova Scotia play for the Canadiens on Saturday night was huge. "I guess I knew that I had some followers [back home] and it made it even that more exciting. I used to love Saturday night hockey. You just knew that everybody was watching. That's one of the things about Montreal I wouldn't have gotten if I had played in Los Angeles or St. Louis: the opportunity for my friends and family to watch me."

Mike McPhee has that classic Mike McPhee look on his rookie: the helmet and the moustache. He had that look for his entire Canadiens career. He had it when he finished up his playing days with the Dallas Stars as well. The back of his card reveals some nice little trivia; part of the bio reads, "Mike notched his first NHL goal, with an assist from Guy Lafleur vs. Edmonton's Grant Fuhr, 3-15-84." Scoring your first goal on a Hall of Famer with an assist from a Hall of Famer is a great way to break into the league. McPhee doesn't recall the details of the goal, but he does remember having a knack for beating Grant Fuhr.

"I don't know why Grant Fuhr was a guy I could score on. Some goalies I couldn't score on, but Grant Fuhr, I think he had a big five hole," says McPhee, who scored 200 career NHL goals. As for the guy who assisted on his first goal, Mike McPhee offers up this nugget. "I've got personal trivia that nobody knows, I've told a few people but Guy Lafleur assisted on my first NHL goal and then I assisted on his last NHL goal in Montreal [as a member of the Canadiens]. It probably doesn't mean quite as much to him as it does to me. To play with him was pretty amazing—a little bit nerve racking at first. My first game was in Detroit and Jacques Lemaire put me with him. And I thought [Lafleur would] be pissed off because he had to play with me on the fourth line. But he actually was pretty gracious about it and came up and just had a little chat with me before the game. I remember him saying, 'Let's get out there. You're here for a reason. Let's get out there and be the best line on the ice tonight.' That was pretty cool."

Two short years later, Mike McPhee helped bring a Stanley Cup to Montreal. His rookie card came out the same year that the Canadiens won that Stanley Cup in 1985–86. McPhee was part of an unexpected Habs Cup run, a big part. He assisted on three of the more memorable goals from that surprising Montreal spring.

First up, Claude Lemieux's Game 7 overtime winner against the Hartford Whalers in round number two. "I was kind of fighting alongside of the net and banked it off the side of the net and Claude was there." Lemieux unleashed a fantastic backhander and beat Mike Liut high on the glove side; the Canadiens were on to the third round. "Claude would always say, 'You just give me the puck. I'm a better goal scorer.'"

Game 3 of the Candiens Stanley Cup semifinal series against the New York Rangers went to overtime. Patrick Roy was sensational that night. He made 44 saves, setting the stage for Lemieux to be the overtime hero once again. Mike McPhee had the puck on the left wing, barrelling towards the Rangers' blue line, and he gave it up for Lemieux. "We had a two on o against the Rangers when he scored that goal. I had to pass it, he was going to go offside," says McPhee.

Montreal took care of the Rangers in five games. Next up was a trip to the finals against the Calgary Flames. Calgary took the first game of the series. The second game of the series, also at the Saddledome, went to overtime. In OT, Mike McPhee assisted on one of the most incredible goals in finals' history. Overtime was over in an instant, it lasted just nine seconds: Brian Skrudland scored the fastest overtime goal in NHL history.

The overtime started with a broken play at centre ice. The next thing he knew, Mike McPhee was on a two-on-one with Skrudland. The only man between the two Canadiens and Calgary goaltender Mike Vernon was McPhee's fellow Bluenoser Al MacInnis. McPhee, on his off wing, hauled back and faked a shot, then sent a perfect feed on to the waiting stick of Skrudland. Skrudland deflected the puck across the goal line in one fluid motion. The game was over. The series was tied at a game a piece. "I know one thing, my dad was getting a drink in the kitchen so he missed it. But I think he's seen it about 50 times since then.

"I keep telling Brian I was dumping it in his corner. I can remember we were probably more excited after that game than after we won [the Cup] because, you know, it was so much of a we had our backs against the wall [scenario]. We had to win that."

McPhee played in the NHL until the end of the 1993–94 season. When his career wrapped up in Dallas, he entered the hockey card game. Mike McPhee, he of the 1985–86 rookie card, was now in the hockey card business with Score/Pinnacle.

"I went into Pinnacle thinking, 'I'm a hockey player. I've collected hockey cards. I've been on the hockey cards. I know something about business.' I remember the VP of marketing, I was kind of giving him my two cents and he stopped me. He said, 'Mike, it doesn't matter what you think. All that matters is what the client thinks.' I hadn't been in the hockey card business but I thought that because I had played

hockey that I knew something about hockey cards and collectors that I really didn't."

Pinnacle used McPhee's input to help create sets. In fact in 1995–96 McPhee picked his own team for a series called "Score Summit." McPhee was basically the GM and he chose his dream team. Gretzky, Messier, Lemieux, MacInnis and others made up the 20-man squad. "I got to pick my own, there weren't any restrictions. I got to pick my team and I tried to get some grinders and some goal scorers and mix it up a little bit." Card number 21 in the set was the GM, Mike McPhee. "I had my own card, in a suit and tie."

The suit and tie were a sign of things to come. McPhee eventually got his MBA and moved from the hockey card business to investment planning. He made some money on the ice and now he's making some money off the ice. And speaking of investments, McPhee still has a few of his old rookie cards, but they didn't make him rich.

"They aren't worth as much as Gretzky's," he says and laughs.

Brian Bellows 1983–84 OPC #167

Looking back on it, Brian Bellows's rookie card is a pretty normal piece of cardboard. The back of the card however tells quite a story, and we'll get to that in a bit. But first, the front.

Brian Bellows doesn't have an outrageous haircut. He is in a very nice uniform. By all appearances, this card is pretty normal. His memories of the time, of the card, are pretty normal as well.

"My first year in the league, the old helmet, I got a black eye. Those things."

In the fall of 1982, Brian Bellows made the jump right from Junior to the NHL. At the start of the 1982 season, Bellows really was a fresh face. He had just turned 18 on September 1st of that year. Age didn't seem to be a problem. He scored an impressive 35 goals in his rookie season to go along with 30 assists for 65 points in 78 games. "We had a veteran team, so enough guys were there to help you. I lived with a family so it wasn't too dramatically different living-wise than being in Junior.

"Al MacAdam was the main guy. He's from Prince Edward Island. We roomed together. He was, I think, the main guy for kind of leading me the right way. I'd go out with him for dinner, we'd room together. He'd just kind of keep you on the straight and narrow. You know, what's expected, what's not expected. Just kind of setting the parameters in a good way.

"Once I got in there I knew I could play. It's kind of a plus and minus. It was good I went to a team that was good. The flip side is you didn't play as much if you go to a team that's poor. It's hard to say whether if I'd played somewhere else if it'd be a different number or not. But you know, I was satisfied [with the rookie season]. Coming in I was thinking I wanted to get 20-plus goals my first year, so I kind of met that."

Bellows set some lofty goals because he put up some lofty numbers as a junior. The back of his rookie card only gives you a mere glimpse into his life in the OHL. Look on the left side: "Bellows scored 3 goals and assisted on 2 others in Kitchener's Memorial Cup Final win in 1982."

What that brief bio does not tell you is that Bellows was on an absolute powerhouse team in Kitchener that year. He led the team in scoring with 97 points. The 1981–82 Kitchener Rangers went 44–21–3 and also boasted two future Hall of Famers on the blue line, Al MacInnis and Scott Stevens.

However there is another great little tidbit on the back of the Bellows rookie card. When you read it, you wonder, "There's no way that can be true, right? That has to be wrong? Somebody pulled a gag?" But it *is* true. The statement in Bellows's bio reads, "While injured at Kitchener, Brian coached 2 games and finished with a 1–1 record." Seriously? An injured 17-year-old stepped behind the bench of a Major Junior team and ran the show? "Back then you only had one coach," Bellows begins, very casually. "Not like now where you have four or five guys. So Joe Crozier [Kitchener's coach] got suspended and he didn't really have anybody and I was injured with a separated shoulder. So he just had me coach. You know, you already know the lines, you know the match ups, you know how things are supposed to go. At the time it didn't seem that crazy. I'm sure if Scotty Stevens was out, he could have easily coached, or Al MacInnis, not a problem at all, because you know the team better than any outside guy."

Could you imagine the headlines something like this would make today? "Injured 17-Year-Old Steps Behind the Bench!" TV stations would be begging the Rangers to let them put a microphone on Bellows for the game. There would be a huge news conference so everyone could get in on what was going through the mind of the 17-year-old coach. Bellows would be on every front page in the country. But all this went down in 1981. It wasn't that big of a deal then. "Back then it's kind of like, well, okay. Yeah, sure. Kind of makes sense? Just roll with it. There's pluses and minuses to all the excess media now."

For the record, Bellows kept things simple behind the bench. "At times you had to do some strategy. If you're down, you gotta play certain guys a little bit more. If you're up, you can spread the wealth around a little bit more. If the game got rougher, you switch tactics there, who's playing, who isn't. You know which guys get more ice time. The guys made it super easy to realize the situation we were in. They were all helping me so that was half the battle right there."

Coach Bellows was sharply dressed too. "I think if I remember correctly, back then we had to wear dress clothes for all the games. So I would have been in at least dress pants and a shirt. Probably that." And of course Coach Bellows was a player's coach. "Well, you gotta play with the guys the next day — so you didn't have much choice."

Brian Bellows went on to eclipse the magical 1,000-point plateau during his 17 season career, ending up with 1,022 NHL career regular season points. He also snagged himself a Stanley Cup with the 1992–93 Montreal Canadiens. He totalled an impressive 15 points in 18 games during the Habs Cup run.

Somewhere along the line the guy on the rookie card started picking up some cardboard of his own. Bellows put together some really impressive stuff, and even owned some of the earliest hockey cards ever made. "Most of the pre-war stuff—Ice Kings—I had. I had a set of C [19]10, '11s and a few other ones like that. Some of them I've gotten rid of. Some of them I haven't.

"I just stopped because prices started taking off. It was fun to collect it when you could get it. But now when you start making investments you have to worry about it. That changes the whole perspective. But it was neat. You knew you had the first whole set ever made. That was really cool. That part was fun."

These days Bellows doesn't invest in hockey cards, but he does work in the investment business in Minnesota. His goals are much the same as they were when he was a rookie: rack up some big numbers. Just like he used to do as a teenage hockey player for the old Minnesota North Stars over three decades ago.

4

SPECIAL COLLECTOR'S CARD

BOBBY ORR

300

Damaged knees have forced Bobby to retire from active hockey at the relatively young age of 30. In a sensational ten year career, Bobby scored 270 goals and assisted on 645 others. He won the Norris Trophy eight times — the Hart Trophy three times and the Art Ross Trophy twice.
Bobby wrote new records for defense with his revolutionary new style and lightning speed. At his retirement press conference, he was called a "living legend" of hockey.

Même s'il n'est âgé que de 30 ans, des blessures aux genoux ont forcé Bobby Orr à prendre sa retraite comme joueur de hockey actif. Durant sa carrière fantastique de dix saisons, Bobby marqua 270 buts et contribua 645 assistances. Il décrocha le Trophée Norris à huit reprises, le Trophée Hart à trois reprises et le Trophée Art Ross deux fois.
Bobby établit plusieurs records comme défenseur, grâce à son style de jeu exceptionnel et a sa vitesse foudroyante. Durant la conférence de presse où il annonça sa retraite, un journaliste déclara qu'il était une "légende vivante" du hockey.

BOBBY ORR 1978–79 OPC #300

One of the great things about my job is that it is a little different every day. When you work at Sportsnet, you never know who is going to drop by the building.

Like every other Canadian kid of the '80s, I grew up not watching, but hearing of the legend that is Bobby Orr. By the time I got my bearings, Orr was retired from the

HALL OF FAMERS

Chapter Eleven

game. I'm sure I watched him at some point in my very early youth, but I was most likely watching number 4 from my playpen.

However, just like everyone else my age, I heard the stories of the legendary number 4. I heard them from my dad. I read about them in old hockey books. I watched Orr at his best when Don Cherry would sneak in a sweet Orr goal on "Coach's Corner." And of course, I saw a lot of Orr in my hockey card collection. All I really needed to know was captured on little thin pieces of cardboard.

That brings us to what many consider the final great moments of Orr's career, the 1976 Canada Cup and card number 300 from O-Pee-Chee's 1978–79 set. There he is, on the bench. Taking it all in. Thinking. Anticipating. No doubt in pain. And waiting. Waiting to make another great play. Waiting to fight off more pain and lead Canada to a win.

Bobby Orr's career ended way too early. Knee injuries took their toll on number 4. After only six games in the 1978–79 season, Bobby Orr was forced to retire at the age of 30.

In its '78–79 set, O-Pee-Chee rolled out a "Special Collector's Card." It did not show Orr pictured during his glory years with the Bruins. It did not show Orr suited up with the Chicago Blackhawks; a couple of air-brushed cards had taken care of that. Instead, O-Pee-Chee went into the archives. They went back to the fall of 1976, to the first ever Canada Cup. Orr left the Bruins after the 1975–76 season. It was a tough year on Orr. In '75–76, injuries limited him to only 10 regular season games. He still put up 18 points. The question for Orr during the summer was: could he play in the Canada Cup? Would he finally get to play in a best-on-best tournament? Surely we'd know who had the greatest hockey nation on Earth after this tournament. The only concern was, would the greatest player on the planet be good to go?

Orr was banged up. The Red and White had been down this road before. Canada had to play the entire '72 Series without the star blue-liner. It couldn't happen again, could it?

Fast-forward 35-plus years and who walks into our Sportsnet studios but Bobby Orr. He was there to talk about a program he's involved with that gives helmets to five-year-old children across Canada. As always, Orr was a pleasure to talk to. Our five-minute on-camera interview flew by. But there was no way I could let Bobby go without talking about this card. He had one more interview lined up but promised me we could talk about the old hockey card.

Orr finished up his final interview of the day, then came straight at me. It was interview time, with number 4, talking about number 300 in the 1978–79 set.

"Oh I know that puppy," says Orr when he glances at a picture of the card. "My dream was to play in the NHL and be on a Stanley Cup team. 1976 certainly is the highlight. It's the only time I played for my country in an international series and that team was unbelievable. And that series is certainly a highlight.

"I was with the team in '72 but didn't play. I wasn't sure if I was going to play in the series ['76]. I wasn't in great shape. I did a little bit of training, short training, but again the team was so good, it was not a difficult series to play in."

Orr is being his ever-modest self here. He finished in a three-way tie for the tournament scoring lead with nine points. And by all accounts, Orr did so while in considerable pain. Orr, however, focuses on the great players he played with in '76 rather than the pain he had to play through. One of those great players on that team has a spot on this classic card; Denis Potvin is on the bench right beside Bobby Orr. Potvin had nine points in the tournament as well. He was part of that three-way tie for the tournament scoring lead alongside Orr and the USSR's Viktor Zhluktov. "Denis is one of my favourite defensemen. In my mind, one of my top ones. Denis was tough. He could play anyway you wanted." Orr continues, giggling at the thought of the talent that team had on the blue line alone. "That defence with Robinson and Savard . . . it was pretty good, pretty good."

And let's not forget about the talent up front: Bobby Hull, Daryl Sittler, Guy Lafleur, Phil Esposito, Marcel Dionne . . . we could go on and on. And of course you can't forget about Rogie Vachon, who put on a great show in the crease. This is crazy to even think about, but 16 of the players on Canada's roster from that 1976 tournament are now in the Hockey Hall of Fame. So of course, we have to ask: if '72 was the greatest moment, was '76 the greatest team? "I'm not going to compare. I think in years to come they'll talk about it as one of the best teams. It was pretty good team. It was a very good team," say Orr.

The 1976 Canada Cup was Orr's last great hurrah. He went on to play just 26 more NHL games over the next three seasons. In fact, he sat out all of '77–78. Thankfully, when the people at O-Pee-Chee decided to pay tribute to Orr when he was forced to retire, they picked one great shot. In his one and only time representing Canada on the international stage, Bobby Orr helped Canada win the first ever Canada Cup and was named tournament MVP in the process. There's a reason you see those stars on the front of the card. Bobby Orr truly was one.

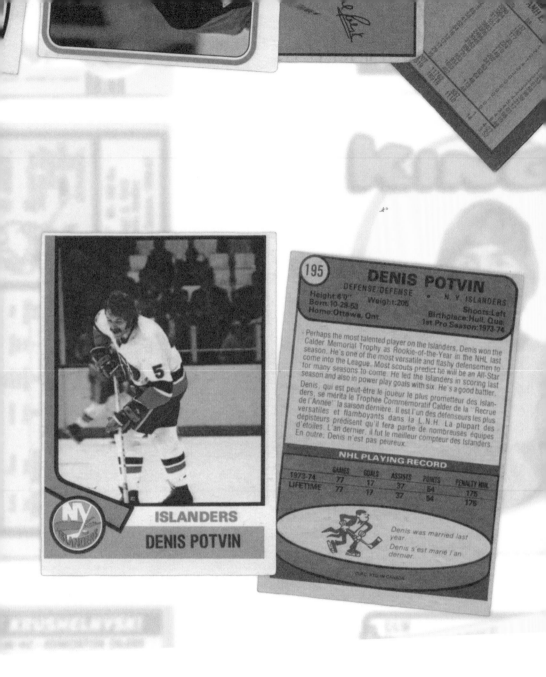

Denis Potvin 1974–75 OPC #195

When it's 1983 and you're a nine-year-old hockey fan, a few things are pretty obvious: no one will ever beat the New York Islanders; Billy Smith is the meanest man on the planet; and no one combined toughness and skill like Denis Potvin.

I run into Denis Potvin every now and then at the office. He still looks like a tough dude. But, man, is he a nice guy. I can't remember him being such a nice fellow back when he was on the ice, but he's always smiling whenever I see him in our Sportsnet studios. I think he looks the way he always did. But he didn't always look the way he always did. Denis Potvin's rookie card defies all Denis Potvin logic.

A quick glance at Denis's rookie card and several thoughts enter my mind, the first of which is: Really? There's no way that's Denis Potvin. The long hair, the 'stache, the sideburns, that can't be Potvin! But most of all, where is it? There's no sign of it. I'm talking about Potvin's trademark Northland helmet. There's no way the guy on the front of this card is Potvin, right?

Wrong, it's all Denis.

"The look was very much the look that I took out of junior hockey. I think in 1973 the Fu Manchu and the almost shoulder-length hair was pretty much in. Wasn't it?" says Potvin. For the record, yes, that look *was* very much in. "I wasn't trying to be a fashionista or anything. I was just trying to blend in, I think," chuckles a man who has to rank on anyone's list of the top defencemen to ever play the game.

Denis Potvin's Hall of Fame NHL career kicked off on Long Island in the fall of 1973. He had just completed a stellar Junior career with the Ottawa 67's. How good was Potvin? Well, he played his first three games with the Ottawa 67's during the 1967–68 season when he was only 14 years old. He returned in the fall of 1968 for his first of five full seasons in Ottawa. When his junior days came to an end, it was decision time for Potvin. Like a lot of players in the '70s, he had a choice: WHA or NHL? The Chicago Cougars held his WHA rights. The New York Islanders took him first overall in the 1973 draft.

Bill Torrey, the boss of the Isles, was a wise man. He made the decision easy for Potvin. In March of 1973, Torrey pulled off a trade with the Philadelphia Flyers. Terry Crisp went to Philly and Jean Potvin, Denis's older brother, along with a player to be named later, went to the Islanders. "Yeah, that pretty much solidified my choice," says Denis of the trade that brought his brother to Long Island. "I just wanted to go to the NHL. And obviously having my brother there meant a big deal as well."

Potvin's Hall of Fame career was underway, so let's get back to the card, and the question. Where is the helmet? Potvin figures the photo was taken during warm up, hence the absence of the Northland. But there was one time that Denis Potvin, who, let's face it, is pretty much Mr. Northland, went into battle without his trademark lid. It all goes back to his first NHL game.

"This is a story that you're getting—I don't know if many people know," begins Potvin. "We went to Atlanta, I think, to play the first game of the season, my first game in the NHL, and when we got to Atlanta we were wearing the dark uniforms, and I guess the trainers opened up the bag and the only helmet I had was the white Northland. So I had to start the game with no helmet on." Potvin was more than just a little nervous. He'd worn a helmet for his entire hockey life and now he was in the rough and tumble NHL of 1973, a rookie with no head protection.

"I'd never played without a helmet, even at the early stages. So I was nervous as all heck. [The trainers] took the time to paint, to tape the helmet. They used black tape. And they put it all around the helmet so that it made it somewhat legal for me to wear in the opposing team's building because we were wearing the dark colours."

It turns out that rookie card isn't all that deceptive after all. Potvin did lace them up in the NHL without a helmet—for 20 minutes at least.

"So if somebody wants to do something on trivia with you and says, 'Did Denis Potvin ever play without a helmet in a real NHL game?' You can say, 'Yeah, sure he did. It was the first period in the first game,'" says the first defenceman to ever reach the 1,000 point mark in the NHL.

This card is proof that cardboard doesn't always capture that classic picture of your favourite player from days gone by. Denis Potvin without a helmet—imagine that? But it's true, on the card, and at least for the opening 20 minutes of his NHL career. By the way, if you want to see that famous Potvin Northland, it's still around, at least the blue version. "I'm very fond of that helmet. One of them is in the Hall of Fame. The white one disappeared. I'm not sure where that went."

At least we're sure it's not on his rookie card.

PHIL ESPOSITO 1971–72 OPC #20

I remember the first time I saw, or at least recall seeing, Phil Esposito. "Man," I thought, "That is one cool dude." Here was a guy in a cool-looking beige suit, strutting out on to the ice to congratulate Wayne Gretzky on setting a new record for most goals in a season. It turns out the guy in the suit had the previous record, 76 goals in a season.

They do not make hockey players like Phil Esposito anymore. I wish they did. He is candid; he's honest. And on the ice he was entertaining. This is a guy who tripped while being introduced during the '72 Series in Moscow, and of course he had fun with it. This is a guy who sings my favourite hockey song, "The Hockey Sock Rock." Once upon a time, while on a book tour, he stopped into the Ottawa TV station I was working at. After our interview the camera guy needed what we call a cutaway shot. That's when you'll see an interviewee and the reporter walking on camera. Phil and I lined up for our cutaway and the next thing I know we're singing "The Hockey Sock Rock." It was a real thrill.

So of course when it came to his hockey cards, Phil was his own guy. Take a look at Esposito's 1971–72 O-Pee-Chee. This set has to have one of the coolest designs of all time. I love the big letters across the top and the round circular pictures on the card. Every card from this set looks like a winner. But take a good look at Espo's card, a really good look. Sure, he's wearing that awesome Bruins uniform. And he has his signature look on the card. But something is a little off. First things first, we all know Phil wore No. 7 for the Bruins. But for some reason, these gloves sport the number 17.

And then there's the one thing that makes this card stand out. That makes it say, "This thing is from the early 1970s." Phil Esposito, one of the greatest goal scorers to ever play the game, the leader of Canada at the 1972 Summit Series, is wearing some of the sweetest slacks you will ever see. I know what you're thinking, "Slacks on a hockey card?" Yes, slacks on a hockey card. Not hockey pants, slacks. Why? The answer is pretty simple. Espo was a busy man and, like always, his own man. He didn't have much time for hockey card picture day. "Eagleson [head of the NHLPA] insisted that we do it because of the players association and if they took pictures of me it was in and out as quickly as possible. Because I thought it was a waste of time," says the always honest and up front Esposito.

And during the winter of 1971–72 when kids were riffling through their packs of hockey cards, maybe coming across this Esposito classic, Esposito was having another classic season on the ice. He scored 66 goals. The previous year he set a new NHL record with 76 goals. Things just clicked for Espo and linemates Wayne Cashman and Ken Hodge.

"Cashman was really good in the corners, and tough. Kenny Hodge was the strongest guy I ever played with or against, and he would be in the other corner or he would be in front of the net, just by the crease. People thought that I was always just in front of the net," Esposito says of a reputation that always stuck with him. "I wasn't. I was up by the hashmarks. I was never really in front of the net except for my last two years in New York because Freddy Shero, that's what he wanted me to do, because nobody else would go there. And I didn't like it, but I went there."

As for that endearing legacy of Esposito camped right out in front of the goaltender on the edge of the crease, he says he doesn't know why it sticks. And frankly, it doesn't really seem to matter to him. "I have no idea, nor do I care," chuckles Esposito. "I know what I did. That's all that matters."

Esposito played during a special time. No helmets, at least for most of the players, and lots of personality. Phil Esposito said what he wanted and he did what he wanted—the man wore slacks on a hockey card! He still says and does what he wants. There aren't a lot of Phil Espositos on the ice anymore. "I wouldn't want to play in this era. No way. In the first place, it's too structured. You can't be an individual. In the second place, these guys have no respect for one another and I wouldn't want to play in this era."

As for those pieces of cardboard, they still don't mean anything to

Esposito. "They don't mean diddly to me." Sure he sees them all the time, but they don't seem to evoke any great emotions. "I go to these shows, people bring me these cards, I look at them and I say, 'My God. Where'd you get this?' I don't see them. I've never looked at them before."

However there is a nostalgic side to Esposito. He still has a few items from his playing days around the house. "I got my 700 goal stick. I got my last pair of hockey gloves and I got the skates I wore from 1973 that I still wear. I got my same equipment from 1972–73 and I still wear it," says Esposito, who spends his winter as part of the Tampa Bay Lightning's broadcast crew.

"Nowadays these guys don't got equipment, they've got armor. These guys are bigger and they're faster. There's no doubt about it. They've got six percent body fat, which means the only thing they can hurt is muscle. In our day, we had a little fat on us. And you didn't hit the muscle," says Esposito. "You had to go through the fat before you could get to the muscle."

So there you have it. One of the greatest goal scorers the game has ever seen is not a hockey card nut. When it came time to pose, Phil did his job. He moved in, smiled for the cameras and if he was wearing slacks, so be it. And maybe he got a few bucks from the card company for his troubles. "If we did, it was 100 dollars or something. Who the hell remembers?" Honest and up front as always, Phil Esposito, just like his 1971–72 O-Pee-Chee, you gotta love it.

Tony ESPOSITO 1969–70 OPC #138

Tony Esposito is one of the greatest and most innovative goalies to ever play the game. On his rookie card he's captured in all his youthful glory in his thick leather pads, donning his heavy glove and blocker and draped in that classic Blackhawks jersey. Tony is striking a pose for all to see. If he looks a little sweaty, there's likely a good reason for it. Tony says he was never quite sure when picture day would arrive.

"In those days they just said, 'I'm going to take your picture,'" says Esposito from his summer home in Wisconsin. The Blackhawks legend says it could have been after practice, before practice, who knows? "It wasn't like a planned deal, you know. It just happened. They didn't set up an appointment. But sometimes they did it after warm-up, or something like that."

Tony Esposito arrived in Chicago for the 1969–70 season. Up until that point he had only appeared in 13 NHL games with the '68–69 Montreal Canadiens. When left unprotected by the Habs in the old reverse draft, he ended up in the Windy City. "Every team protected so many players and I think two goaltenders. And then they had a little draft where the team that finished dead last had first pick. You get it, sort of like the draft. And Chicago had first pick. And Montreal had a choice to protect me, Vachon and Worsley. They decided to protect Vachon and Worsley. Which I think was a great break for me."

Esposito finally had a shot at being a number one goalie, and he grabbed it. The game changing, if not career changing moment, or moments, is right there in print on the back of his rookie card. Beside an awesomely drawn cartoon character of a hockey player slamming a door are the words "Tony shutout the Canadiens twice before this season was two months old."

"I remember the first time because there was me and Denis DeJordy. I started a couple here and there, and Denis played a game in New York and that, and I wasn't clicking in. Not like I thought I could play. And I went into Montreal and we beat them and I got a shutout. I remember that game. I had a pretty decent hockey game and that's when I sort of clicked in and got it going."

Tony Esposito had arrived. Esposito posted an incredible 15 shutouts in '69–70. That number still remains tied for the second highest total in an NHL regular season.

Life was grand. Esposito lived 18 miles, door to door, from the old Chicago Stadium. He'd make his way to the rink in his 1964 Chevy Super Sport. He'd get dressed, put on that classic Blackhawks uniform and hit the Stadium ice with some of the best to ever play the game, including Bobby Hull and Stan Mikita. "That rink was phenomenal," says one half of the legendary Esposito brothers. "You didn't have to worry about getting up for a game. You went in there and it was loud, ohhh, and it was fun." The place was literally smoking. "Sometimes by late in the third period, you'd look up above the glass and you'd see a haze of smoke. Smoke in the building, because in those days there was no law against smoking." It sounds like something straight out of Hollywood. But it was straight out of Chicago. And Tony Esposito lived it.

Following that 1969–70 season, Esposito went on to play 14 more seasons with Chicago. But Tony Esposito wasn't just a goaltender. He was an innovator. He was one of the first goalies to ever consistently leave the stand up position. Nowadays everyone practices, and calls it the butterfly.

"I didn't feel like there was any rule that you had to play a certain way, as long as you stop the puck. So I just tried different things and sort of put it all together and it helped me in my style, because I basically was very fast and a reflex kind of guy so it worked good for me."

Esposito fiddled with his equipment too, adding pieces on to his glove. Most goalies today wear a mask/cage combo. They can thank Tony Esposito for that. "I was getting hit in the eye a few times," Esposito explains. "The third time it affected my vision for half an hour or so. And when it came back I said, 'I got to do something.' I got a real warning

there, you know. I just got one of those caged facemasks and I took the cage off and I got vice grips and a hacksaw. I put it in the vice and I came up with that and then I put it on. I did it myself."

Tony Esposito likes to hold on to things. "I'm a funny guy. I don't get rid of anything." He figures he still has a few of his old rookie cards somewhere around the house. I mention the fact that I just saw one of his rookie cards on eBay, in mint condition, with an asking price of $4,000. "Really? That's a lot of money," says the member of Canada's famous 1972 Summit Series team.

So maybe Esposito has a rookie card or two somewhere in his house. We're not quite sure. However, if you're looking for the ultimate collectable from Tony's first season in Chicago, it's down in Wisconsin. Remember that old 1964 Chevy Super Sport?

"I'm looking out my door right now. It's still here," says Esposito. "I put it away in the late '60s after I got there. I bought another car and I put it away and it looks like brand new." The old Chevy has about 60,000 miles on it. Esposito figures it's worth a lot more than his rookie card. "It's got feather skirts, Hollywood mufflers, my original car. It's beautiful."

And so is that rookie card.

STEVE SHUTT 1974–75 OPC #316

"Hey, that's when I was hot. I was cool then. I'm not so cool anymore," says Steve Shutt when the topic of his more than stylish 1974–75 rookie card comes up.

There he is, a young Steve Shutt on the cusp of greatness. The guy with the sideburns who is just leaning into the frame on this beauty was a high scoring winger from the OHA's Toronto Marlies. The Canadiens drafted Shutt fourth overall in the 1972 draft. He had finally made it in Montreal, huge sideburns and all. That was not an easy task. How tough was it? Shutt recalls his first reaction when he was taken by the historic franchise in '72. "I was a little disappointed in the sense where I said, 'Geez, you know, that team is so strong I'm never going to make the team.' I thought I was going to go to Vancouver but actually Don Lever went there so that was my first thought. I said, 'Geez. I'm going to be, you know, the fifth left winger.' And that's basically what I was."

Steve Shutt had his work cut out for him. As the fifth left winger, he had to fight for ice time. A scorer in Junior, he now also had to learn to play away from the puck. He played 50 games with the Habs in 1972–73 and scored eight goals and added eight assists. Not bad. But Shutt noticed something. He was an NHLer but he still did not have what most NHLers had, a hockey card. The following season, he scored 15 goals in 70 games, still no hockey card. Apparently he had to impress more than just the Habs brass. He also had to impress the card makers if he wanted to become a part of the cardboard world.

"All I know is I was a little upset that I didn't get a rookie card," says Shutt. And he's right. His rookie card is more like his third year card. Shutt had to pay his dues. "It was like, 'Oh well, I'm not in this series [of cards]. What happened?'" Shutt has a theory on why he took so long to make his cardboard debut. He'd pose for pictures during every training camp, just like the rest of the Habs. But come crunch time, he would not end up in a pack of O-Pee-Chee.

"They'd basically just sit there and say, 'You know we have 22 Montreal Canadiens and those are the guys that played here last year so that's the

246

guys that we're going to take,'" says Shutt. "So all of the young guys, you know, they'd take pictures but they wouldn't put them in the series."

Soon enough though, Shutt left the card makers with no choice. He started scoring at an epic rate. 30 goals. 45 goals. And then, in 1976–77, Steve Shutt sniped 60 goals in 80 games. There was no denying it now: this guy would be a regular in wax packs for years to come.

Of course when he scored those 60 goals in '76–77, Shutt also went on to win a Cup with the Habs. That Cup in the spring of '77 was the second of four in a row for the Habs. The Canadiens of the late '70s are widely considered to be one of the greatest teams ever assembled. In particular that '76–77 team that amassed a record of 60–8–12. Yep, eight regulation losses in 80 games.

"As you're doing it, it really is a blur," recalls Shutt of those golden years in Montreal. "Everything is happening so quick. And don't forget, in between those four Cups, there were two Canada Cups. So you know, we never stopped. So it was continuous and just every single day there was something going on. So you didn't have time to really think about all the achievements of the team and what was going on around [you]. Now obviously I've had a couple of years to retire and sit back and think about it and look at it. Then you realize really how great that team was. And you know the best part of it and the reason the team was that good? It's because they literally were a team. You know, who was better, me or Bob Gainey? You know, I scored 50 but Bob stopped 50. We had great defensive players. We had great offensive players. You know, we kind of had specialists in really every role."

Life was grand for Steve Shutt. And it all started a few years before, with fantastic leaning in the frame pose on his 1974–75 rookie card. Light blue background, big sideburns, a shot of a young man about to embark on a tremendous journey. Montreal in the '70s was indeed a magical time. "That was the big style at that time in the '70s," Shutt says when referring to that killer haircut. "Obviously being 20 years old, being part of the Montreal Canadiens, it didn't get any better than that."

Shutt now makes his home in Alabama where he works in the ice business. He's a long way from the flashy nights at the Forum, but he's still close to the game. His company makes sheets of ice for arenas throughout North America—ice that current superstars skate on. Ice that will no doubt make it on to this generation of high tech hockey cards.

"When you look at the old cards, some of the kids look at them and they all laugh, you know. And I say, 'You know, let me pull out some of your pictures when you were 20.' All of a sudden, it's not that funny anymore," says the Hockey Hall of Famer. "Everybody in the world has got some bad pictures and unfortunately some of them, our bad pictures, are on hockey cards."

I guess that all depends on your definition of bad. This card looks pretty awesome to me. The memories of that time will always live on thanks to books, film, storytellers and, of course, thanks to something as simple as a piece of cardboard.

"When I'm dead and gone, my hockey cards will still be here."

But hey, that's all good. As Shutt himself pointed out when we started our conversation, "That's when I was hot."

Bernie Federko 1978–79 OPC #143

Hockey players are athletes, but hockey players are also performers. That's why we pack into arenas across North America, we want to be entertained.

When you look at Bernie Federko's rookie card, you can't help but think the guy is an entertainer. He looks like he is on centre stage without a single soul around him. Federko looks like he is under a spotlight in perhaps the darkest hockey rink in the history of the game. "A lot of the buildings were really dark. Obviously with the technology, the lights in every building are now a lot brighter," says Federko.

Let's face it, most arenas these days are basically just glorified TV studios, built for HD broadcasts. The players are the stars; the fans filling out the seats are basically just the extras. Hockey these days is a grand production. Federko's card, from a simpler era, makes it look like he is the star of a one-man stage play rather than a major HD production.

"You know when I look at that [card] now, it brings back a lot of fond memories. It was a lot of fun playing in that era," says Federko, who racked up 41 points in his first full season with Blues. He had a 31 game cameo with St. Louis in '76–77 before he finally cracked the Blues lineup full time in 1977–78. Shortly thereafter, his rookie card hit the market.

"The first time you see a hockey card of yourself I think that's pretty exciting to see. When I look at other cards, I still think that the Blues jersey of that era; the sweater that we wore until the mid-'80s was still one of the nicest sweaters that there was," recalls Federko of the sweet blue and yellow combo the Blues sported. "I'd like to see the Blues go back to that colour, because I think that was one of the nicest colours and it was always one of the nicest jerseys."

When you flip a card over, you see some pretty cool things. The best thing that stands out to me is Federko's hometown: Foam Lake, Saskatchewan. That just sounds like hockey, doesn't it? Federko's bio also gets right down to the point. It notes he "scored a Goal and an Assist in his 4th NHL game. In his 5th game he topped that performance with a 'hat trick.'" These are the type of things that jump back at Federko when he looks at his first hockey card.

"To know that you've made it, that you're in the NHL and then all of a sudden when you're able to score your first goal [in the Boston Garden against Gerry Cheevers], I think every time I do see that card I think of my rookie season and I really think of scoring that first goal. The first time I got to play in the NHL and scoring a goal in Boston.

"My first home game, I got to play in St. Louis at the old arena, I got a hat trick against the Buffalo Sabres too, so that will be something that I never forget. Just to be able to start your career and playing your first home game and all of a sudden three goals, [it] was a special night for me."

When you look at the early numbers from Federko's career, they are not overwhelming: 64 points in his first 103 games. You may not be thinking that's a Hall of Fame type of start to a career. But soon enough, the man alone in the spotlight on the front of his '78–79 rookie card started to mesh with his mates, two in particular. Federko soon started to skate on a line with Brian Sutter and Wayne Babych. The trio was known as "The Kid Line."

"That era for us with Babych and Sutter was really exciting. Especially '80–81 when we had a really good hockey club," says Federko. In the 1980–81 season, the Blues finished second in the NHL's regular season standings with 107 points. Bernie Federko, then just 24 years old, led the Blues in scoring with 104 points. It was the first time in his career that Federko topped 100 points. He would have four 100-plus point seasons in his career. Federko finished his career with 369 goals, 761 assists and 1,130 points. In 2002, the kid from Foam Lake was inducted into the Hockey Hall of Fame. Having a Hockey Hall of Fame career didn't even enter Federko's mind when he was a young guy on the front of his '78–79 rookie card.

"No, no. Not for a moment. You put on the uniform for the first time, you put on that sweater, it's the greatest thrill just to know that you made it to the National Hockey League . . . you concentrate on trying to stay there. So no, there were no aspirations. I wanted to have a good career. I wanted to be part of a Stanley Cup winning team. And certainly I think that's the biggest disappointment that I wasn't able to do it. I think that's what we all play for is just to get our name on the cup and get a Stanley Cup ring. You know you never had aspirations of being a member of the Hockey Hall of Fame, and that happened. And certainly I'm very proud of that. But it was something that never really entered my mind when I put on that uniform for the first time."

These days Federko still has a lot in common with the Federko on his rookie card. He still makes his living in a rink. And he is still in the spotlight. Federko is part of the St. Louis Blues TV broadcast team. He's an analyst; he is about as close to the game as you can get without playing. He's the first to admit the lighting in rinks around the NHL is a tad better these days. And he's more than pleased to share the game with anyone, be it a viewer or someone who asks about his old hockey cards.

"I have family members that have collected cards for years; people are rabid about collecting. They're rabid about the history of the game, and I think this is what hockey cards are all about. With the history of the game, the players that used to play, by collecting the cards, you really can keep the tradition going for your own family for generations to come by passing the cards down to your kids and then your grandkids."

Exactly, Bernie. And that is really what those tiny little pieces of cardboard are all about. Sure, some of them are worth a lot of money, but for most of us, they are a link to the game's past. And they are a link to our past as well—to a time when there was nothing more important than running down to the corner store and forking over a quarter for the simple thrill of getting a chance to rip open a pack of cards, smell that old gum and get a chance to see your hockey heroes up close.

ACKNOWLEDGEMENTS

First off, I would like to express my gratitude to the men I interviewed for this book. Each and every player, from the Hall of Famer to the guy who skated in a single NHL game, was beyond generous with his time. I thank each of you for talking about an old piece of cardboard and often doing it with a fantastic sense of humour. Just like the sport we all love, without the players, this book would not be possible.

Thank you to my editor, Michael Holmes, and everyone at ECW for taking a chance on this project. From the very first day I entered your office, it has been a first-class experience. Michael, I can never say "thank you" enough for your guidance, professionalism and friendship throughout this entire project. This includes phone calls on the weekend.

How can I even begin to thank my literary agent Brian Wood? You took a chance on what I always thought was a strange idea and here we are. For the record, Brian is a master of the written word; I am not. So Brian, thanks for everything, including the extremely painful initial proofread of this book. As anyone who works with me will tell you, I can spell—I just can't type. Brian, I know I drove you nuts, and an infinite supply of cigars would never be enough thanks.

Hey, Mom—thanks for bringing home that price guide way back

when and fuelling my card craze. I am willing to bet that my mom, Marie, has more passion for card collecting than a lot of dudes wandering the aisles at the weekend card show. Thank you, Mom, for always being there, and that has nothing to do with collecting. And yes, my mom still buys me cards. (Pre-1987 only, Mom, please.)

Thanks, Dad, for keeping most of my collection under your roof while my broadcasting career took me across the country. In fact, when I go back to Dad's, I'm still finding cards. ("I told you they were there, boy.")

In order to do this, I had to lean on a lot of people for help. You know, you can't track everyone down using the web alone . . . So a massive assist goes to Jeff "Palm Isle" Marek for always lending a hand, and for always being there to "hockey geek" it up with me at anytime.

Also, huge thanks to Eric Francis, Justin Van Dette, Jason Gregor, Gordie Dwyer, Gair Maxwell, Wayne Mundey, Jim Jerome, Chris Simpson, Kevin Weekes, Brad Marsh, Craig Clarke and countless NHL and minor pro PR people.

There are many others who helped with this project, either with the book itself or just by keeping me amped up as a card geek. So shout outs to Ian Mendes, Sandy MacKay, Lorne MacLean, Craig and Randy Clarke, B and Jean, Scott Woodgate (for giving me the boost to "just write"), Scott Lewis (who has a great hockey card blog and "gets it"), Jamie Campbell (another guy who "gets" cardboard), Evanka Osmak, Terry Ryan, Tim Micallef, Sid Seixeiro, Jeff Azzopardi, Ryan Moynes, Stephen Brunt, Ric Nattress, Bob McCown (I'll be asking for a plug), Doug MacLean, THE HUTCHMAN, Bob Stauffer, Steve Hogle, Peter Reid, Katie Reid (for not tearing up all my cards) and Grant Roberts. Thanks also to hockeydb.com and hockeyfights.com. And to everyone I didn't/forgot to mention: Thank you too.

I also want to express my gratitude to everyone at Sportsnet. It is a great privilege to be able to work for such a fine company. Thank you to Keith Pelley, Scott Moore, Rob Corte, Steve Cassar, all the producers (that includes you George), everyone at the desk, on the floor, in the control room and on the row for letting me play a part in what is a fantastic product. Without all of you and the platform that Sportsnet provides, this book would not be possible.

And most of all, thank you, Ash and Jacoby. Ash, you are the one who always believes in me and the one who always has my back. You tell me when to push and you tell me when to lay off the gas. I know for a fact that I would never have attempted to do this little project without your support. You make me laugh, cry, smile and love.

And to my little man Jacoby, who I am looking at and smiling at right now as I type this. Your laugh and your eyes make my day and make my life. Hopefully one day, you can say, "Hey, see this old thing, my old man wrote it."

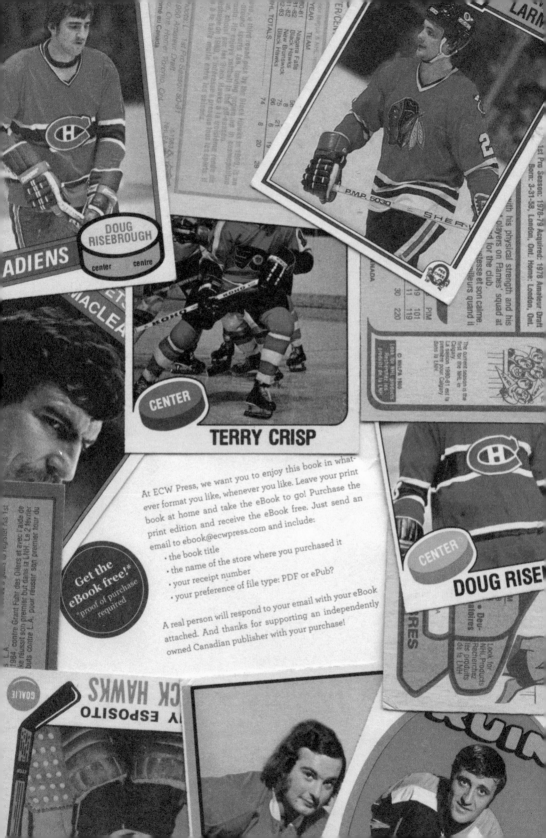

At ECW Press, we want you to enjoy this book in whatever format you like, whenever you like. Leave your print book at home and take the eBook to go! Purchase the print edition and receive the eBook free. Just send an email to ebook@ecwpress.com and include:

- the book title
- the name of the store where you purchased it
- your receipt number
- your preference of file type: PDF or ePub?

A real person will respond to your email with your eBook attached. And thanks for supporting an independently owned Canadian publisher with your purchase!

Get the eBook free!*
*proof of purchase required